What People Are Saying About *Emerge* . . .

"Part river journey, part soul manual—*Emerge* flows with wisdom, awe, and authenticity. Angie Lion shows us how to stop fighting the current and find our way forward."

—Chip Conley, *New York Times* bestselling author and founder of the Modern Elder Academy

"I have known Angie Lion for the past three decades, and her life exemplifies resilience, generosity, and abundance. *Emerge* beautifully captures that spirit. Angie's story and insights remind us that true wealth isn't what we accumulate, but how we live and how we love."

—Jeet Kumar, President & CEO/founder, In Time Tec

"WOW! Angie has written a book that everyone will benefit from reading and sitting with for times of deep reflection. In *Emerge*, she shares her own story of courage, resilience, and growth with a vulnerability that connects the reader to her emotionally . . . this is a great book that I will be giving to many others for years to come."

—Ron Price, author of *The Complete Leader*, founder of Price Associates

"*Emerge* is that rare combination of inspiration and practicality. Angie Lion distills years of experience into clear, actionable frameworks you can apply immediately. Whether you're leading a team, an organization, or simply leading yourself, this book will help you move forward with greater clarity, confidence, and purpose."

—Dr. Jeremy Graves, Dean of the School of Business and Innovation, Ohio Christian University

EMERGE

RISE FROM THE DEPTHS,
REALIGN YOUR *Soul*,
AND RECLAIM WHAT MATTERS

ANGIE LION

Softcover ISBN: 978-1-61206-392-8
eBook ISBN: 978-1-61206-393-5

For more information, visit AngieLion.com

Published by

aloha
PUBLISHING

AlohaPublishing.com

Printed in the United States of America

Contents

INTRODUCTION

The Power of Charting Your Own Course

Welcome to a new beginning. If you've picked up this book, something inside you is already stirring—like the first ripple before a wave. Maybe it's that persistent voice telling you to slow down, look around, and ask yourself, *Is this the direction I actually want to go?* That voice isn't here to nag you. It's here to wake you up.

I get it. I know what it's like to drift along, letting the current of expectations pull you where it wants. For years, I followed a route that was mapped out for me, the so-called *success script* designed by other people. I did what I thought I *should* do, checked all the right boxes, and assumed it would lead to happiness.

But then, life sent me some Class V rapids.

A series of *lifequakes*—moments of loss, upheaval, and challenge—crashed into me, forcing me to grab the oars and start paddling for myself. Those moments made me stop and ask, *Whose map am I even following?* Because it sure as hell wasn't mine.

That's when everything changed. Instead of trying to follow a script that wasn't meant for me, I started reading the water. I learned to trust my instincts, adapt to the obstacles, and row toward what actually mattered to *me*. And now, I want to help you do the same.

You don't need permission from anyone else to chart your own course. You don't have to wait for a crisis to start asking better questions. You can take the oars right now. The only question is . . . are you ready?

WHAT ARE SUCCESS SCRIPTS?

Think about the currents we get caught in. They're everywhere. From the moment we're born, we're swept into streams shaped by family, culture, religion, and society, all of them whispering, "Follow this path. Stay in this lane." These unspoken rules become the undercurrent of our lives, pulling us along without us even realizing it.

These are what many call *success scripts*.

A success script is the set of expectations handed to you—who you should be, what success looks like, and how you're supposed to get there. These scripts shape the course of our lives, telling us to keep paddling in a certain direction, even if it doesn't feel right to us.

For a long time, I thought I was steering my own boat. I thought the choices I made, the career I pursued, and the goals I chased were mine. Some of them were, and some of them were handed to me when I wasn't looking.

It took me some time to see the truth. I had been following someone else's charted route, navigating waters shaped by other people and culture's expectations. Think of it as an *"I'll have what she's having"* approach to life.

Success scripts are the inherited beliefs and expectations that shape our lives, often without us realizing it. These scripts are formed by the influence of family, society, friends, culture, and religion, guiding us to follow a path that may not be our own.

We tend to follow these scripts on "autopilot," driven by a need to fit in, please others, or avoid feeling like an outsider. But these scripts aren't necessarily our truths. They are simply beliefs we've adopted without questioning why.

Rewriting your success script means recognizing which beliefs resonate with you and letting go of those that no longer serve you, giving you the freedom to build a life aligned with your own values and aspirations.

When I was younger, I thought the goal was to "be happy." As a young mom, I told myself that as long as my *kids* were happy, I'd done my job. I didn't realize that I had absorbed one of the most common success scripts: the belief that happiness is a destination. Like so many of us, I believed that if I could just reach the next milestone, land the next achievement, or check the next box, happiness would finally arrive.

But that moment never came—at least not the way I imagined it. Life wasn't waiting with a "just right" Goldilocks moment. Instead, it gave me reality. And that reality included two amazing kids, a struggling marriage, and what I now call my midlife lifequakes or the triple D of *deaths*, *disease*, and *divorce*.

Many of us get caught on the hedonic treadmill of striving for more. That is because we have what scientists call **achieving brains**. And if we don't become aware of it, we are constantly on the chase. Ultimately, these outward goals are no substitute for a larger meaning and purpose. We continue to chase unfulfilling goals that cultivate stress, anxiety, fear, and disconnection.

It was in the middle of that chaos, not after it, that I started to snap out of autopilot and wake up. I started to recognize that our culture has a predefined notion of what constitutes success, encouraging us to seek external validation through possessions, achievements, and connections. It neglects to emphasize the importance of understanding our values and utilizing them as guiding principles in our lives. Moreover, it stigmatizes the very emotions that provide the greatest lessons. Emotions like grief, stress, anxiety, anger, guilt, regret, and disappointment are inherent to the human experience. When acknowledged, they serve as crucial indicators that can guide us back to a sense of self.

It wasn't until the water got rough and I had no choice but to stop and get my bearings that I realized I needed to ask myself some hard questions and take full responsibility for my own journey.

LIFEQUAKES: WHEN YOUR BOAT CAPSIZES

Sometimes, life doesn't give us the luxury of a gentle nudge. It doesn't wait for us to reflect, journal, or gradually ease into change. Instead, it throws us into the ice-cold rapids.

These lifequakes are the sudden storms or the boat unexpectedly taking on water; they are the moments that leave us gasping for air.

A loss, a divorce, a health crisis, or a drastic career change can shake everything we thought was solid and safe. The success scripts we once clung to start to dissolve, and we find ourselves in uncharted waters with no clear direction forward.

For me, a five-year period of intense upheaval forced me to stop drifting. It shook me to my core and made me reevaluate not just what I wanted, but who I wanted to be. I had to ask myself, *Who am I as a being, without the ego and without the scripts?*

FINDING YOUR TRUE NORTH

Charting your own course isn't just looking around one day and all of a sudden deciding to change direction. If it were that easy, you would have done it already and everyone else would be doing it too. The truth is, if you don't know what matters most to you, you'll keep drifting, letting other people's expectations drag you along. The first step to navigating for *yourself* is figuring out what matters most to *you*.

For years, even as I drifted, I still thought I was living according to my own beliefs, making choices that aligned with what I thought I valued. But after my series of lifequakes, when I finally stopped to look around, I realized my values weren't truly mine. I had been steering toward goals I had never actually chosen. To be honest, I really didn't even recognize that I had a choice.

That was my wake-up call.

I had to take a step back and ask myself: *What is important to me? What are the things that light me up, that make me feel alive, that I want to build my life around?* Because if I wasn't clear on that, I would always end up following someone else's map.

If you are serious about rewriting your success script, here's where I want you to start. Yes, before we even dive into chapter one! But don't worry, the goal isn't to finish this exercise before you keep reading. The *Time, Energy, and Financial Audit* is meant to spark awareness that builds over time. You can continue to revisit this exercise as you move through the book or come back to it when something you read later clicks into place.

Open your calendar. Take a glance at your most recent bank statement. Where is your time going? What are you spending money on? These are the parts of your life you're prioritizing, whether you like them or not. If they don't align with the life you want, and you are waiting for a sign, here it is. It's time to stop drifting and start making deliberate choices that put *you* back at the helm.

EXERCISE: TIME, ENERGY, AND FINANCIAL AUDIT

WHAT IS IT?

A *time, energy, and financial audit* is a simple but powerful exercise to help you assess whether your daily actions align with what you truly value. Often, we believe we're living according to our priorities, but our schedules and spending tell a different story. This audit provides a clear snapshot of where your time, energy, and money are actually going, giving you the chance to see if those choices reflect the life you want.

HOW TO DO IT

1. **Identify your top three values**: Take a moment to list the values that matter most to you. These might include family, personal growth, health, creativity, financial stability, sports, or community. Write down your top three so you can refer to them during the audit.

2. **Time audit**: Look at your calendar or planner for the past 6-12 months. Note where your time was spent: screentime and social media, work, family, sports, social obligations, personal development, self-care, etc. Ask yourself: Are these activities aligned with what I value? Did I spend enough time on what I say matters most?

3. **Energy audit**: Reflect on which activities gave you energy and which ones drained you. At the end of each day, rate the day on a scale of 1 to 10 for how it made you feel. Identify the high-energy moments that made you feel alive and the low-energy ones that left you depleted.

4. **Financial audit**: Review your recent bank statements or budget. Are you spending in ways that support your values and goals? For example, if you say personal growth is one of your top values, does your spending reflect that—are you investing in books, courses, or experiences that help you grow? If you say you value family, are you investing in those relationships with your time and money, or are you expecting them to be the only ones to invest time and money into your relationship?

WHY IT MATTERS

The results of this audit might surprise you. When I do this exercise with my coaching clients, they are often shocked to find they are spending time and money on things they didn't realize they were prioritizing. Common surprises include prioritizing social media, kids' travel for sports, entertainment, gadgets, and other external things over what they told me was important to them.

You can identify areas that need adjustment by comparing where you spend your time, energy, and money with your values. If your actions aren't aligned with what you care about, this is your opportunity to make small, intentional changes to bring your life closer to what truly matters most to you.

I encourage you to return to this exercise once you've finished the book to see your progress! It's also a great way to end each year. Use the information gathered in this audit to create your New Year's goals and intentions. Don't beat yourself up when you see the results. Remember, we are building awareness, and once we have awareness, we can start to align our actions with what we want instead of mindlessly following the scripts that have been handed to us.

GROWTH HAPPENS ONE STROKE AT A TIME

Charting your new course doesn't mean flipping your life upside down overnight. You don't just tear up the old map and magically have a perfect new one. This is a process. It is an experiment in learning to navigate differently. Think of it as an expedition, and you are the ultimate explorer.

A lot of us expect change to be fast and dramatic, like some big cinematic moment where everything clicks into place. That's not how it works. Real change happens through small, consistent shifts. It's like paddling against the current. At first, it feels slow, almost imperceptible. But if you keep going, stroke by stroke, eventually you realize you're heading in a whole new direction.

I tell my clients all the time that change can be just a 1% shift. One small step each day, each week, or even each month. If you made a 1% shift each month, by the end of a year, you would be 12% closer to the life you actually want. Now that's making some waves!

Throughout this book, I'll challenge you to explore, experiment, and trust that slow progress is still progress. Your new success script isn't locked in stone. It's a shitty first draft, and every experience you have is an opportunity to refine and adjust. With every little effort, you take control of the flow of life that is truly yours.

AN INVITATION TO EXPLORE

A dear friend of mine recently left her religion, and it completely upended her sense of identity. For years, she followed a success script shaped by her faith community. Her beliefs, routines, and even her self-perception all stemmed from that lens. When she stepped away, it wasn't just the loss of that community that she felt. It was like being set adrift with no map, no compass, and no idea which direction to go next.

She found herself staring at a blank page, uncertain of where to begin or who she even was outside of those expectations.

When we talked, I encouraged her to focus on one thing: exploration. "Try things," I told her. "Volunteer. Join a group. Take a class in something that has always intrigued you. You don't have to know exactly where you're headed, but start paying attention to what brings you peace, excitement, or even just a sense of curiosity."

Rather than rushing to define a new path, I reminded her that she didn't need to have it all figured out right away. Stepping away from one set of expectations doesn't mean you need to immediately replace them with another. This was a time for slowing down, for testing the waters, and for letting her own values and interests gradually lead the way. I encouraged her to try things that helped her find purpose in each day.

"Trust that as you explore, the life you are meant to live will start to take shape," I told her. That's the beauty of charting your own course. Give yourself permission to navigate at your own pace, without the weight of someone else's expectations or validation steering the way. I also encouraged her that just because she had been betrayed and disappointed by her church community, it didn't mean she needed to "throw the baby out with the bathwater."

There are multiple ways to find spirituality and connection with a higher power. I know this to be true through my own personal experience. I told her to start following the love and the light, and reject the old scripts that were replaying in her mind, the ones that used guilt, shame, and fear as a control mechanism.

FINDING YOUR CREW AND TAKING THE FIRST STEP

If there is one thing I know for sure, it's that we are not meant to navigate this journey alone. When I first realized I needed to change course, I didn't do it in isolation. I found people who had charted their own way, mentors who had faced the unknown, and friends who reminded me I wasn't crazy for wanting something different.

Finding your crew is one of the most important steps on the journey.

In the river of life, community is the raft that holds you steady and the fire on shore that welcomes you home. You don't have to navigate the rapids alone. The right people help you stay the course when the current gets strong.

Taking the first step might feel uncertain, but with the right crew beside you, it becomes less about fear and more about flow. Find those who light your path, reflect your values, and remind you who you are when you forget.

So here's my invitation: find a community that supports your journey. Look for spaces where you can explore, connect, and feel free to be yourself. And remember, you don't need to have everything figured out right now. Just keep moving.

THE HEALING POWER OF WATER

Some of my favorite childhood memories are soaked in water—riding my bike for miles just to dive into rivers, leap off pilings, bridges, and cliffs, and spend entire summer days swimming under the sun. My mom, a true water soul herself, had me in the river by the time I was just 6 months old. She believed in the magic of water before she ever knew the science of it—and, in a way, so did I.

Water was where I first felt serenity, freedom, and connection with friends. After my long list of chores was done, I'd slip away and seek out the nearest body of water like it was a sacred refuge. It didn't matter if it was a rushing river, a still pond, or the rhythmic pulse of the ocean. Being near it, in it, or even watching it flow brought a sense of calm and clarity that I couldn't explain back then.

Research shows that water has a measurable impact on our nervous system. The sight, sound, and feel of water triggers what's known as the *blue mind* effect—a mildly meditative state that makes us feel more relaxed, creative, and connected. The sound of waves or a flowing river actually helps lower cortisol levels and increase alpha brainwaves, promoting calm. No wonder I felt so at home there.

Water, for me, has always been more than a backdrop. It's a teacher, a healer, and a mirror. It holds memories of childhood joy, the spirit of my mom, and the stillness I seek when life feels overwhelming. It is no coincidence that so much of my healing, growth, and reflection has also happened near water—and now, through this book, I offer that same current of calm and clarity to you.

In the pages ahead, I'll share stories, insights, and tools to help you navigate the waters of your life. Together, we'll challenge the beliefs that have kept you stuck, celebrate the moments when you choose yourself, and embrace the uncertainty that comes with charting a new course.

You don't need to see the entire river out ahead of you. You need the courage to leave the comfort of the shore. Let go of that old success script, trust your inner guidance and the process, and discover your "soul-filled" self.

How to Use This Book

Each chapter includes practical tools to help you *Emerge*—exercises, Angie's Action Steps, and reflection questions designed to help you rewrite your success script. Think of these as baby steps. These small, intentional actions build momentum and turn into implementation of the concepts we're discussing.

The truth is, I'm still on this journey too. I don't have it all figured out, and I don't expect you to either. My hope is to share what has worked for me so far, knowing that you'll take what resonates, leave what doesn't, and keep moving forward at your own pace.

I chose the imagery on this book's front cover because the river and the chrysalis are two sides of the same story. The river reminds us that life is about movement, flow, and adapting to shifting currents. The chrysalis shows us that transformation requires stillness, patience, and trust in what's forming within. Together, they illustrate that becoming your fullest self is both an active and a reflective process—sometimes you're navigating the waves, and other times you're surrendering to the quiet work of growth.

As such, as you work through these pages, I invite you to:

Own your flaws. See them as proof that you're human and still growing.

Navigate the river. Ask yourself: *How am I going to steer through the twists, currents, and unexpected turns of this journey?*

Step into the chrysalis. Reflect on: *Who am I going to be as I transition and emerge into something new?*

Take your time. Skip around. Come back often. This book will meet you where you are every time.

CHAPTER 1

The Moment Life Calls (and How to Answer)

The year I turned 19, I had what I now call my "appointment with life." I didn't have the words for it then, but looking back, it was the moment everything started to shift. The moment I realized I had a choice.

I was living in a double-wide trailer with my Aunt Babe and Uncle John, two of my biggest supporters. They believed strongly in higher education and had backed me through my first year of college nursing prerequisites. They bought my books, gave me a place to live, and made sure I knew one thing: I was capable of more.

But even with their support, I could feel myself running out of road. I had explored most of what my small hometown had to offer. I didn't like the version of myself that was starting to form—one shaped by comfort, routine, unhealthy habits, and everyone else's expectations and perspective of who they thought I was. I wanted more than the script I saw unfolding around me. I didn't just want to stay afloat in stagnant, reservoir-like waters; I wanted to move forward like a healthy, flourishing river full of life and generativity.

That's the moment life called.

Despite having over two years of experience in home health care and holding a CNA certificate since high school, I was not accepted into my college's nursing program, after applying for two consecutive years. This had been a long-term goal of mine.

I felt like I couldn't catch a break. That door kept staying closed. But instead of seeing that as a dead end, I saw it as a detour and another opportunity, another door. I had already been looking at Boise State University. I had taken some road trips there, and I was ready for a new adventure. I applied for a job at St. Luke's Hospital in downtown Boise as a telemetry clerk to see if they'd call. They did. They hired me and were willing to train and mentor me on their cardiac floor.

And then the letter came: I'd been accepted to BSU.

I packed up my Chevy Cavalier with everything I owned and left behind the only home I'd ever known, my family, my friends, and an incredible boyfriend. I drove eight hours into the unknown to move into a relatively nice apartment with my boyfriend's sister.

I was broke, scared, and had no idea what I was doing, but I was done waiting. I had heard the call, and I was going.

That move to Boise was my first big leap. It was an actual "f*cking first time" (or FFT), a term I picked up from Brené Brown. I was navigating a move (eight hours from home), FAFSA forms, starting a brand-new job, and playing catch-up on some subjects that I'd sort of thrown in the towel on in high school (I'm looking at you, math). I also kept hearing in my head the voice of my high school counselor, who told me I wasn't smart enough to go to nursing school, and I should consider beauty school. I was filled with self-doubt and insecurities.

I was figuring out how to make it all work without a map, without a safety net, and without much emotional, financial, or physical support from my family. But I was resourceful, resilient, and determined. And most of all, I listened to the voice inside me that said, *This isn't all there is. I was meant for more.* So my *don't tell me I can't do something* energy was alive, and it was fueling me.

WHAT IT MEANS TO HAVE AN APPOINTMENT WITH LIFE

An appointment with life is a moment when you feel a shift, and you know that you're being called to something more. For some, it's the realization that the script you've been following no longer fits. For others, it's an opportunity that feels like it was meant just for you, even if it defies logic or the expectations of those around you.

For me, that call started as a restlessness. Over time, it grew into an insatiable curiosity: *What would life be like beyond the edges of this small town? What if I could create a new story for my life?* I knew that if I stayed, I'd continue living a life shaped by default and by others' decisions. But leaving meant stepping into the unknown. It meant taking a leap of faith and trusting that the risk of staying stuck outweighed the risk of trying something new.

Appointments with life can look different for everyone. It might be leaving a job that no longer serves you, moving to a new city or country, or stepping out of a relationship that doesn't bring you joy. It could be deciding to go back to school, start a business, get into politics, or simply saying yes to something you've always dreamed of but never summoned the courage to pursue. For some, it might involve parenting differently than how you were raised or challenging cultural or familial expectations to design your own path.

CHOOSING COURAGE OVER COMFORT

Making the decision to leave wasn't easy. At 19, I packed my car and drove to Boise for college. I had spent my entire life in North Idaho, surrounded by the familiar—family, friends, and routines that felt semi-safe but also limiting. Leaving meant stepping into the unknown. I was excited, and I was also terrified. Yes, both can happen simultaneously, and they show up together quite often.

There's a moment from that day that is burned into my memory. Sitting in my car, gripping the wheel, I knew that I was about to leave everything familiar behind. My stomach was in knots, and my mind was racing with doubts. But beneath all the fear, something had shifted. I knew I had made the right choice.

I wanted to explore new places, meet new people, and experience a life that felt bigger than the one I had known. No one in my family had charted this sort of course. They were comfortable with staying. I was not. In some ways, I felt like a black sheep. In some ways, I felt like a brave explorer. It was empowering and scary as hell all at the same time.

There was no metaphorical map for what lay ahead, and GPS—metaphorical or otherwise—didn't even exist at this time. There were no TikTok or Instagram influencers to share their life hacks with me.

But now I know something that I want to share with you if you are stuck waiting for the conditions to be just right before you take off: *waiting for the perfect plan is just a way to avoid fear and discomfort.*

Growth happens outside of our comfort zones. Bravery happens when you make a choice to move forward even while scared.

Leaving home was my first real act of courage. And that decision continues to shape the person I am today. Along the way, I encountered some truly wonderful people, as well as some mean-spirited individuals, rude people, bullies, and those with ill intentions. It was nothing different from home, but at least at home, I had some comfort in the chaos.

I had to find new coping mechanisms. Sometimes I chose exercise and getting outside on the greenbelt, but other times I turned to distraction and numbing. Unfortunately, the latter was not only unhealthy but also addictive.

But courage isn't the absence of fear; it's choosing to take the next step while fear whispers that staying put would be easier. It's saying yes to charting a new course, even when the outcome is unknown.

THE CHALLENGES OF ANSWERING LIFE'S CALL

The first six to twelve months of any move are the hardest. It's when the initial excitement fades and you're left navigating a new landscape without a map. The routines, people, and comforts you once leaned on are gone, and what replaces them is a mix of emotional waves and limitless possibilities.

There's uncertainty about where you belong, who your people are, and whether this was the right decision. There's fear of being misunderstood, of not finding your footing, of failing in a new place. There's loneliness even in crowded rooms, even when you're technically "fine." There's grief for what you left behind, even if you chose to leave it. There's self-doubt that asks: *Did I make the right move? Am I strong enough for this?*

And there's often a strong desire to turn around. To retreat to what's familiar, even if it no longer fits.

I know those feelings well.

But a few short visits back home helped me remember *why* I left. Not out of rebellion or recklessness, but because I was ready for more. I wanted healing, growth, peace, and possibility.

And sometimes, we have to leave in order to truly see. Sometimes clarity only comes when we return to what once held us and realize it no longer does.

The waters weren't always smooth. In the first couple of years, I hit plenty of rough patches—a plethora of bad decisions, financial struggles, and moments of self-doubt that made me question everything. I juggled part-time jobs, made mistakes in relationships, and even landed on financial aid probation. There were days and long nights when I felt completely lost, wondering if I had answered the right call.

But each of these challenges was a lesson. Every stumble was part of me figuring it out for myself. I learned how to adapt, how to prioritize, and most importantly, how to trust my own instincts instead of letting other people's expectations steer my decisions.

One of the hardest parts of answering life's call is dealing with judgment and confusion from others. Some of my family didn't understand why I needed to leave my hometown. The success script they were familiar with said I should stay, finish school, get married, and settle down. But that script wasn't mine. I had to get comfortable disappointing people who wanted me to follow in a direction that didn't feel right to me. Yes, disappointing people is uncomfortable.

But so is feeling like you're being pulled along against your will, kicking and screaming.

When I first began to navigate these new waters, I leaned on two things: mentors and curiosity. I didn't have all the answers when I left home at 19, but I sought out people who could guide and support me. I found ways to connect. I joined new groups, met people who shared my interests, and put myself in rooms where I could learn from others. I have always been open and willing to learn new ways of being.

The biggest shift, though, came when I started actively asking for help. Most of us resist this because we don't want to feel like a burden or risk rejection. But here's the truth: people generally *want* to help if we are brave enough to ask.

So, here's my advice. Don't hesitate to reach out. Find people who inspire you, who have been down a similar river, or who make you feel safe. Be clear about what you need—whether it's guidance, encouragement, or just a listening ear. And if someone says no, don't take it personally, and keep asking. The right people are out there.

You don't need to have every step figured out to move forward once you've answered life's call. Sometimes, just asking the right person for help is enough to set everything else into motion.

WHAT IT MEANS TO ANSWER LIFE'S CALL

Answering life's call is rarely the easy or obvious choice. You have to listen to the whispers of your soul and take action, even when it feels risky or uncertain. For me, I had to step out of the success script I was handed and begin to write one of my own.

Looking back, I realize that every appointment with life brings a choice: will you say yes and leap into the unknown, or will you stay rooted in the safety of the familiar? There's no right or wrong answer, but there's always a cost. The cost of staying is often the regret of what might have been, while the cost of leaping is the discomfort of uncertainty and fear of failure.

EXERCISE: RECOGNIZING LIFE'S CALL

Life's call often comes in whispers, not shouts. Here's how to recognize it:

- **Discomfort**: You feel restless or uneasy in your current situation.

- **Daydreams**: You find yourself fantasizing about a different life, job, or future.

- **Opportunities**: A chance to do something new appears, but it feels scary.

- **Voices of support**: People you trust encourage you to explore something outside your comfort zone.

Ask yourself, *Is there an area of my life where I feel a pull toward change? What would it look like to lean into that feeling?*

EVERYONE HAS AN APPOINTMENT WITH LIFE

At some point, life will tap you on the shoulder and ask you to stop and pay attention. For some, this shows up as a major turning point, like walking away from a career that no longer fulfills you, packing up and starting fresh in a new city, or choosing to leave a relationship that is literally crushing your soul.

The choice is always yours. But the sooner you stop numbing, distracting yourself, and ignoring it, the sooner you start moving toward the life you are meant to live.

Growth requires risk. Staying where it feels safe might be comfortable, but it often comes at the cost of your potential and your overall sense of peace. One of the hardest lessons I've learned is that you can't grow and stay comfortable at the same time.

The most meaningful changes in life happen when you push past the limits of what feels safe and step into the unknown.

Fear shows up every time you step into something new. That feeling is normal. But I've also learned that fear is often a signpost that you're on the right track.

If you've answered the call and fear is showing up, take it as a sign that you're heading in the right direction. Fear doesn't mean you made the wrong choice. Action kills fear. The river doesn't stay calm when you leave the shore. It moves faster, carving a new path. That rush of uncertainty? It's proof that you're growing and that you are alive. Keep going. Trust the current. You're exactly where you're supposed to be.

LISTENING TO YOUR INNER VOICE

Fear is part of the journey, but so is trust. Trust in yourself. Trust in your ability to navigate uncertainty. Trust in that voice inside you that already knows the way forward. If fear is the rushing current, your intuition is the steady flow beneath it, guiding you toward the life that is meant for you.

That inner voice nudging you toward something more can be easy to ignore when it's drowned out by the expectations of others. But it's always there, waiting for you to listen.

Your intuition is one of the most powerful tools you have when it comes to rewriting your success script. For me, listening to my inner voice has meant pausing and reflecting during life's transitions to ask myself hard questions: *What am I pretending not to know here? Am I doing this because it aligns with my values, or because it's what others expect of me? Is this decision bringing me closer to the person I want to be? Am I expecting someone else to save me?*

If you want to hear that voice more clearly, you have to create space for it. That might mean journaling, taking a walk, or just sitting in silence for a few minutes. Your intuition will guide you if you give it the chance.

And here's the thing. When something feels *off*, it's because it probably is. That discomfort, that nagging feeling that you're meant for something different, is not random. It's your inner compass pointing you in a new direction. Trust it. Trust yourself. The first step toward building a life that feels real and aligned is listening to the part of you that already knows. I'll say it again: action kills fear.

ANGIE'S ACTION STEP

Identify one area where you've been hesitating, holding back, or waiting for the "right time." Is there a conversation you need to have? A decision you've been avoiding? A step toward something bigger that you've been too afraid to take?

Do something about it today, even if it's small. Make the call. Send the email. Say *yes* to the opportunity that scares you. Take one intentional step that moves you closer to the life you know you're meant to live.

And if doubt creeps in, ask yourself, *If I don't act on this today, will I regret it in five years? Ten?*

Regret can be a powerful signpost of what matters to you and where life is calling you to grow.

As you consider these questions, remember: the success script you're living right now isn't set in stone. You have the power to rewrite it. All it takes is the courage to start. Give yourself permission. Allow yourself to flow.

REFLECTION QUESTIONS: YOUR APPOINTMENT WITH LIFE

At the end of each chapter, you'll find a set of reflection questions designed to help you engage more deeply with the ideas we've explored.

Take a moment to pause, write, or simply sit with these prompts. Use them as a tool for self-discovery and a guide for charting new waters.

🦋 Write about a time when you felt called to something more but ignored it. What held you back?

🦋 Think about your life right now. Is there an area where you feel a quiet pull for change?

🦋 What is one small action you could take today to explore that calling?

CHAPTER 2

Facing Resistance

Moving to Boise was my decision. No one pushed me. I went because I felt called. I wanted more for my life, and that meant leaving my small town and the predictable path I saw unfolding if I stayed.

I had followed my intuition, and I had taken the leap. Maybe my early days of cliff jumping and diving had built some transferable skills for overcoming fears in regular life, too.

But within a year, the waters started getting a little rougher. The freedom I loved so much started bleeding into recklessness. I was making poor choices, self-sabotaging, partying too much, and losing my grip on the version of myself I had hoped to become. I started regressing. This is what I refer to as my "cringey Angie" phase of life. My boyfriend and I broke up due to the nature of long-distance relationships. Then, I didn't get into the nursing program at Boise State.

My roommate and I shared the single life of our early 20s with wide eyes and open hearts. We laughed hard, cried often, and took long drives up the scenic route from southern Idaho to the panhandle—always with a fresh playlist, big dreams, baskets of laundry in the backseat, and some Girl Scout cookies for the trip.

We met Roman and Kevin, new friends who quickly became part of our weekly rhythm. Roman showed interest in me early on, but I initially saw him as just a friend. Over time, that shifted. We grew close while spending days on the ski hill during winter (we both worked one day a week at a ski resort for the free season pass) and camping and adventuring in the summers. What started as a friendship evolved into something deeper.

Eventually, my roommate finished college and moved back to her hometown. I moved in with another roommate for a while in a cute duplex, and for a moment, life felt stable again—until it didn't. My relationship with Roman came to an end, and just like that, I lost my partner and another roommate in the same breath.

The life call I'd worked so hard to answer began to unravel.

I moved back home to the double-wide trailer I'd shared with my Aunt Babe and Uncle John. I went back to the local college to finish my associate's degree. And I felt like a complete failure.

Then, in the middle of winter, Roman showed up at my door, telling me he had made a terrible mistake and asking if we could try again. I was all in. On April 2, 1995, we were engaged. By June, we were married. We were both 22, and I felt like he was my Prince Charming.

When I told my Uncle John about the engagement, he was furious. The man who had helped raise me and my little brother Andrew, who had always been in my corner, looked me dead in the eyes and told me I was going to turn out to be "stupid white trash" just like the rest of the family. He said he wouldn't be at my wedding, that I was throwing my life away. That once I got married, I'd never finish school and I wasn't welcome in his home anymore.

What he didn't realize was that his resistance added fuel to my fire. I was determined to prove him wrong not out of spite, but to prove to myself that I could still chart my own course and create a life worth living. I didn't drop out. I didn't give up. My new husband and I got jobs that winter and moved back to Boise together. And brick by brick, we started building a future together.

That season taught me something I've never forgotten: people will have opinions—loud ones—about how you live your life. Sometimes they'll mean well. Sometimes they'll be way off base. But their emotions, their beliefs, their fears? That's their business, not yours.

You are the only one who has to live with the choices you make and don't make. Even when you get it wrong—and I've gotten it wrong plenty—you will learn more from your mistakes than you ever will from playing it safe to please someone else. Resentment is a powerful emotion that signals to you that you might be saying yes to things you know you don't want to do. Then the tendency is to blame others for how we feel. I know this cycle very well. It's an easy place to get stuck, kind of like an eddy on the river where you keep going in circles, getting nowhere fast.

When you chart your own course, expect resistance. Expect some people to panic. Expect people to project their fears onto you. Expect some to ghost you altogether. But chart it anyway.

This is your river to navigate.

Along with success scripts, many of us also inherit **scripts about emotions**. These scripts tell us how we're supposed to feel or express emotions. For instance, I grew up in a family where conflict wasn't openly addressed. It was often swept under the rug to avoid discomfort. Conversely, anger was an acceptable emotion in my family, and I learned that as long as I could get angry, I wasn't weak. These scripts taught me to suppress my feelings for the sake of keeping the peace or completely losing it on someone just to win an argument. As I've grown, I've learned that this approach leads to unresolved tension, misunderstandings, and has left me not really liking myself. What feels good in the moment doesn't always feel good later.

Rewriting your emotional script means giving yourself permission to feel and express all of your emotions without shame. Break the cycle of silence and embrace honesty in your relationships. When I finally started sharing my feelings, whether it was disappointment, frustration, hurt, or even joy, it deepened my connections with others and helped me navigate resistance more effectively. Just remember that not everyone can meet you where you are. People can only meet you as deeply as they have met themselves.

THE REALITY OF RESISTANCE

Resistance often comes from the people closest to us. Parents, siblings, friends, and mentors (the folks who love you the most) can unintentionally become the very barriers we have to push through.

For me, my Uncle John's harsh words planted seeds of doubt and made me question my worth. For weeks, I wrestled with the fear that maybe he was right. Maybe I was jeopardizing my future by following my heart.

When someone you care about questions your choices, it can feel like they're questioning *you*. I admired and respected my uncle, which made his criticism cut even deeper. It forced me to confront doubts I wasn't prepared to face. But over time, I realized something critical.

My identity couldn't be defined by other people's fears.

Every time I felt his resistance I used it as an opportunity to get clear on who I truly was and what I wanted. And here's the thing about resistance: it usually has nothing to do with *you*. People's doubts, opinions, and concerns are often shaped by their own fears, experiences, regrets, or unfulfilled dreams.

My uncle's resistance wasn't really about me. It was about his fear. His definition of success and stability didn't match the life I was building, and that disconnect scared him. His reaction to me was based in fear. He knew what often happens to women who can't support themselves and rely on a rescue from their version of Prince Charming. At the time, I didn't know this, but now I see why he responded to me the way he did. He didn't have the emotional intelligence skills to share his fears with me. He just exploded on me. He was afraid that I may be taken advantage of or that someone might use money as power over me if I didn't have a way to support myself. Understanding his reaction took me years to uncover. That didn't make the resistance disappear, but it changed how I responded to it.

Not everyone will see the vision you have for your life. And that's okay. Your job isn't to make them comfortable, to justify, or to make excuses. It's to keep moving forward, even when they don't yet understand the direction you're heading.

EXERCISE: RECOGNIZING RESISTANCE

Resistance can take many forms. Resistance doesn't always come from family (although it often does!). It can show up in your workplace when colleagues don't understand your decision to move on, among friends, or when societal expectations press you to conform to a certain timeline or definition of success. Recognizing resistance in all forms helps you filter what's valuable wisdom and what's simply noise.

Here are a few ways it might show up:

- **Doubt**: "Are you sure this is the right choice?"

- **Fear**: "What if it doesn't work out and you fail?"

- **Guilt**: "Why would you leave us?"

- **Judgment**: "That's not how things are done in this family."

- **Shame**: "Who do you think you are? What makes you so special?"

When you encounter resistance, take a step back and ask yourself, *Is this resistance about me, or does it have more to do with this person's own fears and expectations for themself? Are they projecting their fears onto me?*

Just because someone is questioning your decisions doesn't mean your decisions are taking you in the wrong direction.

TAKING OWNERSHIP

Facing resistance isn't about proving a point. In fact, the more I grow, the less I want to prove myself and the more I want to **improve** myself. It really comes down to taking ownership of my own life. The scripts I had been handed weren't necessarily wrong, but they weren't *mine*. And that meant I had a choice to either keep following a script that didn't fit or start writing one that did.

That choice didn't come without discomfort. Disagreeing with people I loved was one of the hardest things I had done. At first, saying, *I appreciate your concern, but this is my decision*, felt unnatural. But every time I said it, I took back a little more control over my own life.

Resistance stopped feeling like something to fight against and started looking more like confirmation that the path ahead was truly mine and not someone else's.

So, I kept moving forward. I got married. I went back to school. I built a life I could be proud of. My uncle didn't attend my wedding, and for years, our relationship was strained. He had, as he called it, a "hot Italian temper." He never apologized. But eventually, he saw that my husband and I were committed to our education and future, and creating a better life for our kids. Time softened his resistance and he eventually became a huge part of our lives and the lives of our children.

But the biggest shift didn't come from him. It came from me.

For a long time, I carried his words with me like a straitjacket on my soul. I felt the need to defend my choices, to prove something. But over time, I realized that holding onto resentment was just another way of letting someone else's expectations control me.

So, I chose to let it go. I surrendered.

For me, forgiveness wasn't about agreeing with him. It wasn't about pretending his words hadn't hurt and that he hadn't been an ass. He had. All these things were true. It was more about freeing *myself*. When I stopped carrying that anger, I had more space for peace, more energy for the life I was building, and more clarity about the person I wanted to be, regardless of the words he had spoken in anger.

Forgiveness is an undercurrent in the river of life, flowing steadily beneath all experiences, waiting to heal and restore. Every major religion stresses the need to forgive others to free oneself. The choice is always there for you. But that doesn't mean it isn't hard. If it were easy, everyone would do it much more often.

HOW TO NAVIGATE RESISTANCE

When you're navigating the expectations of others, you can't ignore them entirely. Instead, you have to learn to filter their input and decide what's worth keeping and what you need to let go of. Here are a few strategies that worked for me, and I encourage you to try:

LISTEN, BUT DON'T ABSORB

It's okay to hear others' concerns, but don't let their fears dictate your decisions. Think of it as a window into the perspective of that person, similar to data. It's one perspective, and that is it.

I learned this lesson when my uncle's criticisms started to weigh on me. At first, I internalized his words, replaying them in my mind and letting them erode my confidence.

But I realized that his fears didn't have to become mine. By practicing active listening—acknowledging his perspective without letting it dominate my thoughts—I was able to create emotional distance. A useful mantra I adopted was, "I hear you, and I choose to trust myself."

FIND TRUSTED ALLIES

During this period, I leaned heavily on a few trusted friends and mentors who shared my excitement about building a future on my terms. They reminded me of my strengths when doubts crept in and celebrated my wins, no matter how small.

One friend would always say, "You're not alone in this. I'm proud of you for following your heart." Their belief in me helped to counterbalance the negativity I faced from my internal and external resistance.

Seek out people who support your vision and can provide encouragement when you need it most.

STAY GROUNDED IN YOUR "WHY"

I often revisited the vision I had for my life: a partnership built on mutual respect and shared goals, even if it didn't fit the traditional timeline. When resistance feels overwhelming, I've found it helpful to write my "why" on a sticky note or keep it somewhere visible, like on a mirror, my phone, or in a journal. Seeing it regularly reminds me of the bigger picture and helps drown out the noise of doubt.

When doubts creep in, return to the reasons you made your decision in the first place.

PRACTICE SELF-COMPASSION

There were times when guilt about disappointing my family weighed heavily on me. I had to learn to forgive myself for not meeting their expectations and recognize that their disappointment was not my responsibility to fix. Self-compassion has become one of my lifelines. Taking time to journal, meditate, and simply acknowledge my feelings without judgment allowed me to navigate resistance with grace.

It's natural to feel doubt or guilt when facing resistance. Remind yourself that it's okay to prioritize your dreams and recognize that failures are part of the process.

ANGIE'S ACTION STEP

Think about a time when you faced resistance while pursuing something important to you. What did that resistance look like, and how did it make you feel? Now, consider how you responded. Did you hold firm, or did you let the expectations of others sway you?

Identify ways you can prepare to navigate resistance in the future. For example:

- Identify your "safe" people who will support you no matter what.

- Create a mantra to repeat when doubt arises (e.g., "This is my life, and I'm allowed to write my own script.").

BONUS ACTION: PRACTICE FORGIVENESS

Write down someone whose resistance has hurt you. Reflect on what that resistance says about their fears or expectations for themselves. Then, write a short statement of forgiveness—not for their sake, but for yours. For example: *I release the hurt caused by [person's name] because I value my peace and freedom to move forward.*

For me, facing resistance has taught me to honor my dreams, respect others, and stay true to the script I'm continuing to write for myself. It's shown me that the river of life isn't always calm. There are going to be rapids and obstacles, but there's also beauty in the journey. The only way forward is to accept the ebbs and flows that happen when other people's expectations get thrown in the mix and trust in your ability to navigate each turn.

REFLECTION QUESTIONS: NAVIGATING RESISTANCE

Take some time to explore the following prompts:

🦋 Who in your life has the strongest influence on your decisions? How do their expectations align or conflict with your own values?

🦋 What is one area of your life where you feel resistance right now? How might you approach it differently?

🦋 Imagine you could rewrite your success script without any outside influence. What would it look like?

🦋 What would you do if you weren't scared or money wasn't an issue?

Resistance is inevitable,
but it doesn't have to define your journey.

CHAPTER 3

The Lifequakes

Everything was falling into place. I had navigated my family's resistance, proved I could have it all, and was moving forward in my education and career. I had two beautiful kids, a nice home, and life felt like it was on an upward trajectory. Then came an opportunity that felt like the cherry on top—we moved to China.

Living in China was, in many ways, a dream. It was a vibrant, once-in-a-lifetime experience. In a place where nearly everyone we interacted with was an expat, there was an instant sense of belonging. The international schools and communities were warm and welcoming. Friendships formed fast, the connections were deep, and the support system was unlike anything I had ever known. Every day brought new adventures, new perspectives, and a sense of excitement that made life feel full.

But even before we moved, cracks had already started forming beneath the surface.

My marriage had been struggling, and moving to China felt like a fresh start, a chance to reset and rebuild. But no amount of change in scenery or habitat could fix what was broken inside of both of us.

And I didn't see it yet, but I was standing on the edge of a series of lifequakes.

Lifequakes. The word itself evokes upheaval, chaos, and sudden shifts. I use this word when describing those moments when everything you've built starts to crumble, when the ground beneath you shakes so violently that the success script you've been following completely shatters. Suddenly, you have no choice but to start from scratch.

A lifequake might be losing someone you love, a health crisis, a career collapse, or, in my case, a series of overlapping challenges that forced me to question everything I thought I knew about myself.

A **lifequake** is a significant disruptive event that shakes up the plans or "script" you've created for your life. These events can be external, like the loss of a loved one or a career shift, or internal, such as a profound change in personal priorities or values. Lifequakes compel reflection, adaptation, and often a complete reevaluation of your path. They can also serve as catalysts for realignment and growth.

MY FIVE-YEAR LIFEQUAKE

One lifequake would have been enough to shake me. But I didn't get just one. I got a series of them—repatriation back to the U.S., the sudden deaths of both my parents, navigating my Aunt Babe's Alzheimer's and eventual death, and a divorce. Each one shattered my world and my plans.

REDISCOVERING HOME

After nearly three years in China, we came back to the U.S. I thought it would feel like a homecoming. I thought the familiarity would be comforting. Instead, it felt like stepping into a life that no longer fit.

We went right back to the same house, the same neighborhood, the same routines. The same ruts we had left. But *we* weren't the same. Living abroad had changed us. Our perspectives had expanded, our priorities had shifted, but everything at home had stayed exactly as we left it. It felt like I was trying to put a square peg in a round hole.

Repatriation was disorienting and isolating. In China, we had been surrounded by a tight-knit expat community where friendships formed fast and deep. Now that I was back home again, I felt lonely in a way I hadn't expected. And on top of that, I was overwhelmed by thoughts of *What now? Who am I now?*

For those years abroad, I had lived with a sense of freedom I hadn't felt before. I trained for triathlons, learned photography, read books for fun, and found joy in simply *being*. But back in the grind, it all started slipping away. I was back in the striving culture. The financial burdens, the expectations, the responsibilities, and the weight of real life settled back in. I was back in a deep rut, and I couldn't see a way out.

To make matters worse, the problems we had run from during our years abroad began to resurface. I knew that the relationship with my husband wasn't working for either of us.

Repatriation forced us to confront the cracks in our marriage and the reality that a fresh start in a different country hadn't fixed what was broken.

And now, there was nowhere left to hide or escape to, no way to distract myself or numb the pain that was bubbling up inside of me.

A PAINFUL GOODBYE

Shortly after we returned home, life hit me with another blow. When I went to pick my mom up for a doctor's appointment one day, I found her on the floor, too weak to get up. She was admitted to the hospital, where doctors told me she was malnourished due to complications from gastric bypass surgery. On top of that, she had accidentally overdosed by combining her fentanyl patch with oral hydrocodone.

I called my cousin Susan and asked her to come to Boise. My mom looked like a corpse. For several days, it was touch and go. She was delusional about her condition and believed she could still live on her own. In reality, she wasn't paying bills, couldn't manage basic tasks, and her mental health was worsening. She'd made me her power of attorney, and I had to make some really hard decisions.

The hospital recommended transferring her to another facility to stabilize her mentally and physically. I agreed. I couldn't care for her, work, and raise my kids all at once. She was furious, calling family members to say I was doing this to her on purpose. It was heartbreaking. Some family members judged me, but didn't show up to help or support me. I felt alone and betrayed.

Within a couple of months, her condition improved. She was medicated, diagnosed with bipolar disorder, and agreed to enter a rehab facility. She had contracted MRSA and was still weak, so we remained concerned about her medications. But she was happier there. Soon after, she asked me to help her move into an apartment near Spokane. I told her I'd help her move if she found the place herself. I needed to set boundaries because otherwise she would expect me to do everything for her. She eventually did move, and we supported her transition back to independent living.

Not long after, I got a call that changed everything. I was at Roman's dad's cabin with no cell service. When the landline rang, I knew it was serious. My cousin Susan told me that my mom was septic. The hospital would keep her on life support just long enough for my brother Andrew and me to say goodbye.

The winding drive from the cabin to the Boise airport, without cell service, is one I'll never forget. Once I had a signal, I called my brother and a friend to book us on the first flight to Spokane to join our sisters at our mom's bedside. In my frantic packing, I accidentally brought lotion in my carry-on and got searched at security. I didn't handle it well. My brother was shocked—he'd never seen me like that—but our mom was dying, and I was desperate to be with her.

In her final moments of life, our mom was surrounded by people who loved her. She heard our voices and tried to pull out her tube to speak, but she couldn't. Her organs were failing. We stayed with her during her final two days—playing music, brushing her hair, taking turns curling up beside her in bed. We let her know how much she was loved.

On the morning of April 26, 2009, as we shared our favorite memories, her monitors began to alarm. I looked at my sister Michelle, a hospice nurse, and we both knew. It was time. Her heart rate dropped, and she flatlined with a single tear slipping from her eye. She passed peacefully, surrounded by love.

Even in that peace, nothing could prepare me for the grief of losing her when she was only 52 years old. I hadn't expected it. Our family has a history of surviving the impossible. We've beaten stage four cancers and shocked doctors with our resilience. In our family, we have always joked, "You can't kill a Perry." But eventually, we all take our last breath. I just never thought hers would come so soon.

As I wrote this book, I had just turned 52 myself. The weight of that parallel is impossible to ignore.

Grief upended everything. Like all lifequakes, it reordered my world. And as I tried to navigate the loss of my mother, I was also watching my marriage unravel in real-time. The more I grieved, the more distant my husband and I became. The more we drifted apart, the worse everything felt.

Losing my mom was devastating. But grieving her while standing on the crumbling foundation of my life? That broke me.

LAYERS OF GRIEF

Then, two years after my mother passed, life hit me with another phone call that changed my life. Ironically, I was back at St. Luke's hospital for work this time when I got a call from my Uncle Ted. He said, "Hi Angie, I have some bad news for you. Your dad passed away last night in his sleep from a heart attack." My dad and his latest wife were snowbirds in Arizona. He was only 62 and had no signs of bad health aside from being a heavy drinker and a smoker.

Losing him so soon after my mom was another painful lifequake and another crack in the foundation of everything I thought I could rely on. Thankfully, my sisters and I navigated that grief together. We honored him the way he would've wanted, with a big celebration of life, karaoke, and his favorite song, "Remember When" by Alan Jackson. To this day, that song takes us all right back to the love we shared.

Around the same time, my Aunt Babe, my hero and the woman I had looked up to my entire life, was officially diagnosed with Alzheimer's. She had been showing signs of dementia for the past couple of years. The disease started to steal her mind, and I was assigned to step in as her power of attorney. Just as I had done for my mother, I found myself managing her long-term care, her finances, the selling of her property, and the heartbreaking reality of watching someone I loved and really needed slowly fade away. It was an overwhelming grief and heartbreak.

There's a saying that the eyes are the window to the soul, but Alzheimer's clouds that window. I'll never forget what it felt like to sit across from Babe and see her eyes go distant. She would look right at me, but I could tell she wasn't really there. I visited often, hoping for those rare, flickering moments of clarity. And sometimes, miraculously, they came.

I will never forget one of those moments.

It was after I had lost my mom. Then my dad. Then I had to place Babe in a skilled nursing facility because her behaviors were worsening, and they were worried she would escape and get lost. I was barely holding it together. I had just made the very difficult decision that I was going to leave my marriage, and the grief, fear, and shame were swallowing me whole. I didn't know who to turn to. So, I went to Babe for some counsel.

I held her hands, sat beside her, and poured my heart out with tears falling and voice shaking. I told her I was going to divorce my husband, I didn't know what came next and I felt like I was failing everyone. I didn't even know if she could hear me, but I needed to say it out loud.

And then, for just a moment, she looked up. Her eyes locked with mine, and I knew she was there. Really there. She held my gaze and said, "Well, at least you and the kids won't have to salute when he walks in the door anymore."

I laughed through the tears, because that one line told me everything. It told me she saw me. She saw our struggles. That she had seen more than I thought. And that in her own fierce, no-nonsense way, she was giving me her blessing.

But even with that moment of grace, the weight of everything I was carrying didn't go away. My husband wasn't equipped to handle the depth of my grief. I don't say that to criticize him. I say it because it was my reality. Most of the emotional, logistical, and financial responsibility fell on my shoulders. And while I was trying to make it look like I had it all together on the outside, I was broken inside.

A LIVING GRIEF

Divorce is one of the hardest challenges I've ever faced because it's a grief that doesn't have the same closure as death. It's mourning the loss of a life you built, while the person you built it with still exists, just no longer with you.

Like most everyone who gets married, I hoped my marriage would last forever. I was going to do it better than the broken marriages scattered among my family. I was going to break the cycle.

At the time, I didn't realize that I was also falling for the *exceptionalism fallacy*, the flawed belief that I would be the exception, that the patterns and pitfalls I'd seen in others wouldn't apply to me. Most people don't even recognize it, but this can be one of our biggest internal obstacles. It feeds perfectionism and convinces us that if we just try harder or do it "right," we'll escape the pain others couldn't.

But that's not how life works. Marriage requires two people who are equally committed to staying together. And if one person decides they're done, or they don't want to work on it, or they want to blame the other person, it just doesn't work.

Real life doesn't follow the fairy tales we grew up with. You start with the best intentions. You marry the person you think is your forever, build a family, and imagine a future of joy and stability. But then midlife happens. Parents get sick. Kids take over your world. You juggle sports, school, careers, and a million tiny responsibilities that chip away at the foundation you once thought was solid. Somewhere along the way, without even realizing it, the distance and the divide grow. The cracks form, and there is a moat between you and the prince or princess.

For me, that unraveling was devastating. I had believed in my script. I was going to do it *better* than my parents. I wasn't going to get divorced. I was going to have the perfect family.

Striving for perfection can become an addiction. It feels addictive for a few reasons:

- **Neurochemical reward**: Like gambling or social media, perfectionism taps into reward systems in the brain.

- **Control mechanism**: It provides an illusion of control in uncertain or painful circumstances, especially for people with trauma histories.

- **Identity hook**: Many people unknowingly attach their identity and self-worth to performance, making the pursuit of perfection feel non-negotiable.

What makes it dangerous is that the goalpost keeps moving. No matter how "perfect" something is, it rarely brings lasting peace, only more pressure. It can lead to burnout, anxiety, strained relationships, procrastination, and a profound disconnection from joy and authenticity.

But as I navigated loss after loss, the final rumble—the last in a series of lifequakes—was the one that brought my entire world crashing down.

On September 13, 2014, Aunt Babe passed away after weeks without eating and days without water. Unlike my mom's death, I wasn't with her when she passed. I had been there day after day watching her deteriorate, hoping that each day would end her suffering and that I would get the call so I wouldn't have to go back to see her like this another day. It was excruciatingly painful and each day was dreadful.

Losing her was another blow stacked on top of so many others. I had barely processed the death of my parents and was adjusting to life in a divorced family when I had to say goodbye to the woman who had shaped so much of who I was.

The series of losses reshaped how I saw the world and my place in it. And underneath the emotional strain, there was another reality: the financial toll. Navigating end-of-life care, arranging funerals, and managing estates three times in such a short span nearly broke me.

I had been holding it all together, but I was running out of strength. And just like that, I was on the bottom of Maslow's hierarchy, grasping at survival.

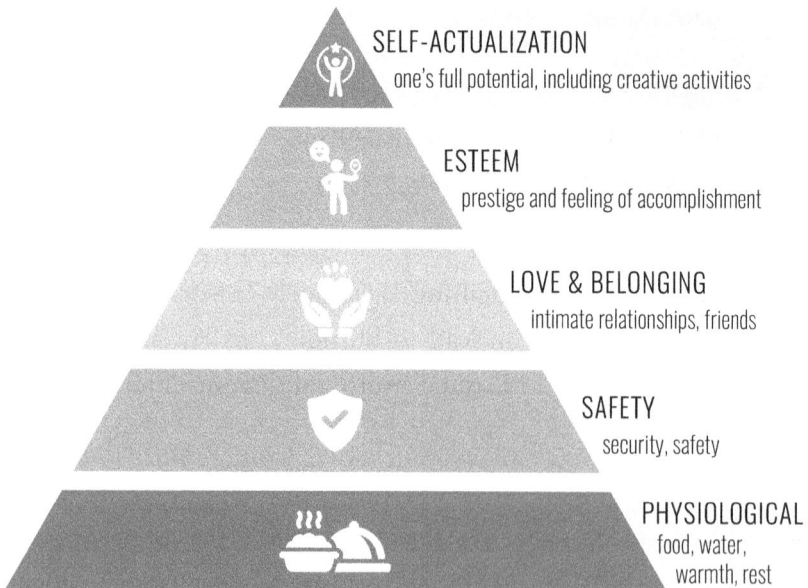

SELF-ACTUALIZATION
one's full potential, including creative activities

ESTEEM
prestige and feeling of accomplishment

LOVE & BELONGING
intimate relationships, friends

SAFETY
security, safety

PHYSIOLOGICAL
food, water, warmth, rest

When our basic physiological or safety needs are not being met, when we are navigating the aftermath of a seismic event like grief, illness, job loss, or trauma, talking about purpose or self-actualization can feel irrelevant and even insulting. In those moments, we are not climbing the pyramid; we are clinging to the bottom rungs, doing everything we can to survive. And yet, this is where I often see a disconnect: well-intentioned leaders at the top of the organizational hierarchy completely missing the reality that some of their team members are barely holding it together.

I have witnessed this firsthand with students, employees, and even clients, when encouragement to reflect on higher-level goals fell flat or created unnecessary shame, simply because they were not in a place to engage with those questions. Context matters. Timing matters. Empathy matters.

So, let me ask you: Where are you on the pyramid right now? Have you ever been at the top, only to find yourself suddenly at the bottom again, like an unexpected slide in a real life game of Chutes and Ladders?

Awareness of where you're at is the first step towards giving yourself grace.

REBUILDING FROM THE RUBBLE

The aftermath of a lifequake doesn't settle immediately. Just like an earthquake, there are aftershocks which cause ripples of disruption that can last long after the initial impact. You can't rebuild yet. You just have to hold on. Protect yourself. Let the waves of discomfort wash over you.

For about five years, I found myself in survival mode, bracing against the aftershocks while still grappling with the magnitude of everything I had lost.

And it wasn't just me experiencing these aftershocks. My kids were navigating their own challenges. When it comes to divorce, the aftershocks for kids last forever, and I felt their struggles deeply as Roman and I tried to rebuild a sense of stability for all of us. Roman and I have set aside our differences for the sake of our children. We maintain mutual respect, and while our connection has diminished, our love as individuals and for our children surpasses any personal conflicts. While we handled our divorce as best we could, there was and still is devastation. It hurt my kids in ways that I wish they didn't have to endure.

Eventually though, the quakes quieted, and I began to see the possibilities in what at first glance had looked like complete destruction.

The rubble began to look like a blank slate and my opportunity to start anew.

Those first steps were small but significant. I leaned on the people who actually stuck by me in my worst of times. These connections helped me start clearing out the rubble to make way for a new foundation and to know that I wouldn't be defined by losses but by the resilience I had gained. I started to see this circumstance as an opportunity to transform my life into something new.

HOW TO NAVIGATE A LIFEQUAKE

A lifequake will knock you sideways. It will take the script you've been following, rip it up, and leave you standing in the wreckage, wondering what the hell just happened. It's overwhelming. It's painful. And it's also an invitation.

Because here's the truth: Lifequakes will come. It's not a matter of if; it's a matter of when. All of us will lose people we love.

> ## Lifequakes force us to wake up, realign, and rebuild in a way we never would have otherwise.

So if you're in the messy middle of lifequake, here's my advice.

First, stop trying to fix everything at once. The aftershocks will keep coming, and the more you fight them, the harder they hit. Acknowledge the chaos, but don't rush to put the pieces back together overnight. Give yourself permission to sit in the uncertainty for a while. Let the dust settle. That's where clarity starts.

Next, focus on who is in your corner. When everything falls apart, the people who truly support you become crystal clear. Pay attention to who shows up. Those connections are your anchors. Lean on them. Let them remind you that even if you feel lost, you're not alone.

And finally, trust that something will come from this. Lifequakes shake everything loose, but in doing so, they reveal what actually matters. They strip away the distractions, the expectations, the things that were never really yours to begin with. What's left? A chance to rebuild on *your* terms.

Here is the truth without the sugarcoating: every lifequake I've been through has been hard as hell. Seismic events continue to have aftershocks long after the initial event. But every single one has been an invitation. A chance to create something new. An opportunity to step into a life that's more aligned, more authentic, and more *me*. While I was hustling and striving, life was chipping away at all the parts that weren't part of my true essence. It was excruciating, uncomfortable, but also necessary.

LIFEQUAKE LESSONS

- **Lifequakes are inevitable but transformative**: As painful as they are, lifequakes are an invitation to reevaluate whether your boat is pointed in the right direction. They strip away the nonessential and challenge you to rebuild with intention. These moments force you to ask, *What do I really value? Who do I want to be on the other side of this?*

- **How you handle crises shapes your future**: The strength of the success script you write after a lifequake is determined by how you navigate the crisis. Will you cling to the old out of fear, or will you embrace the opportunity to create something new?

- **Rebuilding requires both grief and action**: Grieve your old script, but don't stop there. Begin crafting a future that aligns with who you've become. You can honor the past without staying stuck in it. Grieve, yes, but also ask, *What can I create from here?*

A NEW FOUNDATION

After the lifequakes that brought my world crashing down, I began the slow process of rebuilding. It wasn't an instant transformation but a deliberate effort to address both the practical and emotional challenges in my life. At first, I was at the bottom of Maslow's hierarchy, just trying to meet my most basic needs. I slowly managed to work my way back up that infamous pyramid one step at a time.

A huge step for me was being able to support myself and my kids financially. This was priority number one. I was working a part-time job three days a week at a college. Within six months, my role expanded, and they created a new position for me as a Clinical Coordinator. Before this, I had been working part-time with a plastic surgeon but quickly realized it wasn't a stable gig. When the surgeon took time off, I was forced to take time off. When a patient canceled surgery—whether due to illness or not following the no food and water directive—I didn't get paid. I needed steady, reliable work with benefits and consistent pay. The new role at the college offered both, and that sense of security was invaluable as I navigated the aftermath of everything I'd been through. The job became a cornerstone of my rebuilding process, providing not just financial stability but also a renewed sense of purpose and accomplishment through meaningful work and a supportive community.

At the same time, I began to reevaluate my priorities and redefine what success meant to me. Moving up Maslow's hierarchy meant not only meeting basic needs but also striving for connection, growth, and eventually self-actualization.

This chapter of my life wasn't about putting those same pieces back together after they'd all come crumbling down. I had to build something completely new from scratch. I needed to build something that aligned more closely with who I was becoming. The challenges I had faced taught me resilience. And this new foundation would lay the groundwork for my future.

THE REBOUND

As many codependent people do after a divorce, I ended up in a rebound relationship with someone who wore a mask to fit the person I wanted. Let me explain. For the first time in my life, I was thrust into the online dating world. I created a Match.com account, and it wasn't long before I realized the dating pool was shallow and murky. No one looked like the online profile they had created. People do exactly what they do in the hiring process. They play a role.

I went on some hilarious and scary dates, which made me start questioning who I was and what kind of partner I wanted to share my life with. It wasn't long before I was being courted by someone who liked me and wanted me to be exclusive with him. He showered me with gifts and material possessions, which I was not accustomed to. Within no time, he wanted my daughter and me to move in with him. He convinced me that this was a way I could better financially support my son, who was in college at the time. He had a large home, and my daughter would have her own master bedroom and bathroom. I would no longer have to struggle financially. I would be back on top of Maslow's hierarchy!

Then, he bought me my very own horse (something I had wanted since I was a little girl). He took me on lavish vacations. He bought me a brand-new luxury vehicle. He gave me unlimited credit cards to decorate his house because I wanted it to feel homier.

Within a few months of living together and traveling together, I could see that the mask he was wearing was, in fact, a mask. He had darker issues and behaviors that did not align with me or my values, but I mistakenly fell for potential. I stayed long enough to collect enough red flags to make an entire quilt! The ones I didn't collect, I painted green, making excuses for his behaviors that I knew were deal-breakers. My soul knew this the whole time, but once again, I was falling for the prince while still trying to figure out who I was. I was trying on new identities, as if I were the lead in my life's theater.

This was a long detour that I could have avoided. But this detour and this teacher also taught me two valuable lessons:

1. I can't be bought.
2. If it costs my soul, it's too expensive.

This wasn't another failure or failed relationship. I was tempted by my old script, but it wasn't long before I saw this "failure" experience as one of my greatest successes and teachings. I had finally listened to my soul, and I dodged a bullet! To me, that is a success! If I learn a valuable lesson that I can apply in another area of my life or help someone else, to me, that is a success. I can choose to see it how I want. This is often referred to as reframing and it is a powerful tool when implementing an "I either win or I learn" mindset.

ANGIE'S ACTION STEP

Think about a recent lifequake. Maybe you lost a job, faced a health crisis, or experienced the end of a significant relationship. Perhaps this is happening *right now,* or you are still experiencing aftershocks.

Now, take a moment to reflect on how you can use the experience of this lifequake to build something new. Here are three steps to get started:

1. **Identify what's been lost**: Write down what you've let go of or what was taken away during your lifequake. Acknowledge the grief but also the freedom that comes with it.

2. **Reconnect with your values**: Ask yourself, *What matters most to me* now? *How have my priorities shifted because of this experience?*

3. **Take one small, intentional step**: Choose one action that aligns with your new script. It doesn't have to be big—just a single step forward.

REFLECTION QUESTIONS: REBUILDING AFTER LOSS

Take some time to explore the following prompts:

🦋 Write about a time when everything came crashing down, and in the aftermath, you were forced to pause and reflect. What was the lifequake that triggered it?

🦋 What beliefs, routines, or expectations fell apart during that time? How did they no longer serve you?

🦋 Imagine you're writing a new success script after a significant loss. What does the first chapter look like?

CHAPTER 4

Living BIG

After a lifequake, once the dust settles, you're faced with both an opportunity and a choice. This is the moment where you take back control and decide, *What comes next?*

Some people come into your life serendipitously, and you have no idea they'll end up becoming a huge part of your story. That's exactly what happened when I met my now-husband, Rob.

Rob and I first crossed paths years ago during a new teacher's bootcamp he was facilitating. At the time, we were in different places in life. But over the years, we built a friendship.

I was juggling full-time work with part-time studies. Rob consistently offered encouragement and saw potential I couldn't yet recognize in myself. When my next lifequake occurred and I found myself navigating significant life changes, including concerns about completing my degree, his advice proved invaluable. Rather than suggesting I abandon my educational goals entirely, he encouraged me to adjust my course load and stay the path toward my degree.

When Rob faced his own major life transition, we found ourselves becoming important sources of encouragement for each other during a time when we both needed it most.

As we experience lifequakes, new opportunities can present themselves. Sometimes ones we didn't even expect. Soon, we began building something new together. We purchased a home, launched a business partnership, and married in 2018. I relocated to begin this unexpected but welcome chapter of life.

Charting these new waters has meant being intentional about *how* I want to live moving forward. For me, that meant learning to *live BIG*, a concept introduced to me by Brené Brown that became a guiding framework in my life. BIG stands for boundaries, integrity, and generosity, and it helped me create a life that aligns with my values.

As I moved forward, I made a decision to look at all the ways I had allowed other people's expectations to shape my decisions. Setting boundaries and staying true to my values gave structure to my new path. Like water carving new channels, generosity washed away what no longer served and opened space for ease and growth.

PROTECTING MY ENERGY

The first piece of living BIG is learning to set boundaries. For much of my life, I was a people pleaser. I said "yes" when I wanted to say "no." I avoided hard conversations to keep the peace. But that came at a high cost: resentment. I learned that resentment is often a flashing red light telling you that a boundary has been crossed, or in my case, never even created.

Resentment is an emotional signal that something isn't right. It often arises when you've said "yes" to something you didn't truly want to do, ignored your own needs, or failed to set a necessary boundary. It's your inner voice telling you that you've compromised your values or overextended yourself. It's like a check engine light that indicates to you that something you are doing isn't sustainable.

How resentment shows up:

- **Overwhelm**: Taking on too many responsibilities and feeling drained.

- **Regret**: Wishing you had said "no" to something that didn't align with your priorities.

- **Bitterness**: Harboring frustration toward others for not recognizing your limits or needs.

- **Victimhood**: Blaming others instead of doing your work and setting reasonable boundaries and expectations.

Resentment was a sign that I wasn't setting boundaries. I would say "yes" to things out of guilt or fear of disappointing others, and then I'd feel miserable and overwhelmed.

I'll never forget the holiday season when I realized just how much resentment I had been carrying. I was driving home after yet another whirlwind family visit, feeling completely drained, and I asked myself, *Why am I doing this?* The answer was clear: I was afraid of disappointing people. But the cost of that fear was my own peace of mind. That moment became a turning point for me. I knew something or someone had to change. That someone was me. I now refer to myself as a "recovering people pleaser." It took me a lot of years to learn that the word no is a complete sentence. While I still care deeply about others and my relationships are invaluable to me, they can't come at the cost of harboring resentment. When it festers, it creates a kind of stagnation you can feel and smell from a mile away.

Setting boundaries around family expectations has been an important learning experience. Like many couples who move away from their hometowns, Rob and I found ourselves navigating unspoken expectations about always being the ones to travel for visits. The pattern of packing up and making multiple long trips each year to see extended family had become both financially and emotionally draining.

We decided to establish a new approach: alternating years for family visits and focusing on truly meaningful events like milestone celebrations. As expected with any boundary change, this wasn't initially well-received. There were some complaints and pushback, but eventually people adjusted, and we found greater peace in how we were managing our time and financial resources.

Boundary setting is a skill that requires careful calibration, finding the line between protecting yourself and maintaining important relationships. It's one of those life paradoxes that takes practice to navigate well.

This shift allowed us to be more present during the visits we did make. Rather than rushing to accommodate everyone while arriving exhausted, we could genuinely engage and enjoy our time together. It reinforced an important lesson about how thoughtful boundaries can actually strengthen relationships rather than damage them.

BOUNDARIES ARE AN ACT OF LOVE

Many people think of boundaries as walls meant to keep others out, but that's not helpful in any of our relationships. Boundaries are bridges and they show others how to treat you while protecting your emotional energy and well-being. Brené Brown reminds us that "clear is kind."

Communicating what you're okay with and what you are not is an act of self-love and respect.

For me, boundaries became a necessity when I realized how often I said yes just to avoid disappointing others. I would volunteer for extra responsibilities, stretch myself thin, and then feel overwhelmed, burned out, and resentful. This was an obstacle I was creating in my own life and then getting mad at other people for my lack of boundaries. In other words, I was self-sabotaging.

When you set boundaries, you're not just taking care of yourself, you're teaching others how to care for you, too. And while boundaries might create discomfort at first, they ultimately lead to healthier, more respectful relationships. One thing that is important for new boundary setters to know is that you also need to respect other people's boundaries. It is not enough to wall yourself inside your boundaries and then bulldoze over other people or fail to be clear with them about what is okay and what is not. Remember clear is kind and a lack of clarity is not setting anyone up for success in relationships.

EXERCISE: THE BOUNDARY TEST

One simple exercise I've found helpful is what I call the *boundary test*. Before committing to something, I ask myself:

1. Is this a *hell* yes or just a yes?

2. Am I saying yes to please someone else?

3. Will this decision leave me feeling more fulfilled or more drained?

My answers make it clear when that yes should actually be a no or a "not at this time". Some things need to wait until you graduate, until you are off one board and before you join another, until you aren't on PTA, fundraising, room mother, and team mom.

CHOOSING COURAGE OVER COMFORT

The second piece of living BIG is integrity. For years, I ignored my inner voice that whispered, *This isn't working.* I stayed in a marriage that no longer felt right. I made poor choices that didn't align with my values. Instead of trusting myself, I let fear make the decisions. Fear of judgment. Fear of the unknown. Fear of being seen as selfish. I told myself that staying quiet, avoiding conflict, and sticking it out was the *right* thing to do. But I was slowly dying inside.

Silence comes at a cost. Each time I ignored what I knew deep down, it felt like a small betrayal of myself. That feeling built over time, growing heavier until it was impossible to carry. Avoiding hard choices didn't make them go away, it just made me lose myself and not respect myself in the process. It's tough to live with yourself when you don't respect yourself. It's hard to escape you. Because everywhere you go, there you are!

Eventually, something had to give. I had to stop prioritizing comfort over courage.

UNDERSTANDING INTEGRITY

Integrity means making choices that reflect your values, even when those choices are uncomfortable. It requires honesty with yourself and the willingness to take action when you recognize that something in your life is out of alignment. I was out of integrity and out of alignment in a big way.

Integrity often requires us to face difficult truths about ourselves and our lives. For me, this realization came when my brother, who was in a 12-step recovery program at the time, said something that changed my perspective on my life. He told me, "At some point, Angie, you're no longer a victim. You're a volunteer." Those words hit me like a punch to the gut. They forced me to confront the uncomfortable truth: I wasn't living in integrity. I was staying in situations that didn't serve me, not because I couldn't leave, but because I was too afraid to. I was in complaining mode for far too long, and I was also trying to control everything and everyone around me because I had no control over myself. Control was an intoxicating illusion for me that kept me distracted and miserable for far too many years.

And here's the thing: most of us don't recognize the difference between being a planner and being a controller. We convince ourselves we're just being responsible. But beneath all that planning, we're often grasping for a sense of control that doesn't actually exist. What do we really control, anyway? Not other people. Not outcomes. Not the unexpected. Sometimes, control is just a facade we cling to when we're actually falling apart on the inside. And that control creates tension with the people around us, too. When we live that way long enough, it becomes a barrier to integrity.

THE ROLE OF COURAGE IN INTEGRITY

Choosing courage over comfort is one of the hardest choices you'll ever make, but it's also one of the most rewarding. It means speaking up when it's easier to stay quiet. It means making decisions that others won't always understand. It means being willing to let people down if it means staying true to yourself.

Leaving my 18-year marriage was terrifying. I didn't want to hurt anyone, and I didn't have all the answers. There were no guarantees. But staying meant continuing to betray myself and my husband, and that was no longer an option. The pain of leaving had finally become less than the pain of staying.

This wasn't a decision I made lightly. It came after a long season of deep reflection and conversations with people I trusted, both those who were still married and those who had gone through divorce. I kept returning to one question inspired by Matthew 16:26 (KJV): *For what is a man profited, if he shall gain the whole world, and lose his own soul?*

I asked myself: Would my kids rather see me happy and healthy, modeling a loving, functional relationship or watch me stay stuck in dysfunction and pass that down to them? If I left, it might mean continuing the cycle of divorce. But if I stayed and we never grew or healed, weren't we also modeling a cycle we couldn't break? And was I really measuring success by the number of years I had stayed married?

Over the years, I've seen too many people stay in marriages far beyond their expiration date, becoming bitter, spiteful versions of themselves. I didn't want that to be me. That wasn't a "success script" I could live with. I saw myself becoming increasingly resentful, increasingly withdrawn, and I knew that wasn't good for me, my husband, or our kids. It required radical honesty and an unflinching look at myself and the future I was shaping.

Now, as someone who often works with women and young adults, I hear stories of children who are angry with their moms for staying in toxic relationships and letting them grow up in an environment where financial, emotional, or even physical abuse was present. I've also spoken with older women who regret staying in unhealthy marriages, only to watch their children repeat the same harmful patterns.

Yes, control and abuse happen to men as well. But for many women, leaving a toxic relationship carries an extra layer of difficulty: child-rearing responsibilities, financial vulnerability, and the emotional burden of being the family's anchor. Often, women are the primary caregivers, which limits their ability to work full-time or pursue financial independence. The fear of instability for themselves and their children can be paralyzing. When a woman is already stretched thin emotionally, physically, and financially, the risks of leaving can feel greater than the pain of staying. Especially when there's no strong support system or access to resources like childcare, housing, or legal help.

I chose courage, not because it was easy, but because it was necessary.

While the road wasn't smooth, leaving my marriage led me to a life that feels far more authentic and fulfilling. I know I am showing up as a better person for my kids now than I ever could have before, and my hope is that they can forgive me for the pain that I caused in my unhealed journey and all of the mistakes and poor choices I made in those stages of my life.

Now, I want to be clear that I'm not a promoter of divorce. If both partners are willing to do the work, there's something to build on. But if abuse, control, or power over you are part of the pattern, seek help. Remember, you can't change anyone but yourself. People only change when they want to. As Mel Robbins says, "If people want to change, they will. You can't make them."

EXERCISE: RECOGNIZING WHEN YOU'RE OUT OF ALIGNMENT

We all stray from our values at times. The key is to notice when it's happening and take steps to realign. For me, the signs are clear:

- **Restlessness**: A nagging feeling that something isn't right.

- **Regret**: Wishing I had spoken up or acted differently.

- **Discomfort**: Feeling uneasy about a choice I've made.

- **Shame**: A paralyzing feeling. It sounds like you are a failure, you are stupid, you are a joke, you are going to be alone forever, you will never amount to anything.

When these difficult feelings arise, they're not always easy to sit with. It takes practice to allow them to wash over you like waves. Over time, this has become easier for me. Now, I use those feelings as signals to pause, reflect, and make adjustments.

You don't have to be perfect. Living in integrity doesn't mean never making mistakes. It means being willing to take responsibility when you do. It means recognizing when your actions or reactions don't align with your values and making amends when necessary.

Being accountable also means being willing to apologize. A real, honest apology is a skill, and it may take practice to develop. It's something I'm still working on. Here are some practical ways to make more authentic apologies:

SAY THIS INSTEAD: A GUIDE TO MORE AUTHENTIC APOLOGIES

If you're tempted to say this . . .	Try saying this instead . . .
"I'm sorry you feel that way."	"I'm sorry for what I did. I see how it hurt you."
"That wasn't my intention."	"Even though that wasn't my intention, I take responsibility for the impact."
"Let's just move on."	"I want to make things right before we move forward."
"Nobody's perfect."	"I messed up, and I'm learning from this."
"I said I was sorry, what more do you want?"	"I understand that rebuilding trust takes time. I'm here for that."
"You're too sensitive."	"Your feelings are valid. I want to understand your experience better."

SPACE AND GRACE

The third piece of living BIG is generosity with others and with yourself. Generosity means showing up with compassion, extending empathy, and giving people the benefit of the doubt. It's about practicing what I call "space and grace," a mindset that allows relationships to flourish, even in difficult times.

Generosity goes beyond simply giving your time, money, or energy. It means allowing people the space to be human—to struggle, make mistakes, and grow without fear of judgment. Kindness, empathy, and connection create far more impact than criticism or withdrawal.

It is important to note that generosity doesn't mean allowing others to take advantage of you. It works hand in hand with boundaries, ensuring you give from a place of strength and not obligation.

The first time I realized the transformative power of "space and grace" was during a conversation with a friend who was struggling in her new relationship. Her partner was experiencing a lifequake—losing a parent while navigating immense professional stress—and had emotionally withdrawn. She felt hurt and unsure of how to proceed. Based on past experiences, she saw this behavior from him as a rejection of her.

I asked her one simple question:
"Can you give him some space and grace?"

Those words shifted her perspective. She began to see that his behavior wasn't about her, it was about his pain. By offering him the space to grieve and the grace to process his emotions, she stopped taking his withdrawal personally. Instead, she chose to show up for him in a way that respected both his needs and her own.

This mindset didn't just preserve their relationship; it deepened it. It allowed her to support him with compassion while maintaining her own emotional boundaries.

GENEROSITY IS A CHOICE

Generosity is a conscious decision to see the humanity in others. When someone lashes out, generosity allows you to step back, think, and get curious: *What might they be going through?* When someone disappoints you, generosity reminds you to offer grace instead of holding a grudge or being a judge. It's not easy because judgment is often the easiest route. It takes work (time, energy, and thoughtfulness) to ask questions and try to see things from someone else's perspective. If it were easy, everyone would be doing it.

As Brené Brown puts it, "Generosity is assuming positive intent." That doesn't mean ignoring harmful behavior, but it does mean pausing to consider the full picture before reacting. Dr. Ellen Langer beautifully explains, "the behavior makes sense to the actor; otherwise, they wouldn't be doing it." The behavior is also only the tip of the iceberg that we see on the surface. We don't see a million other emotions, thoughts, circumstances, and beliefs that are swirling around under the surface.

Generosity also extends to yourself. Often, we're hardest on ourselves, holding ourselves to impossible standards while offering grace to everyone else. Learning to be generous with yourself—to forgive your mistakes, honor your needs, and let go of self-judgment—is just as crucial as extending that grace to others. I might even go so far as to say that it is *more* important. It's hard to escape yourself. Remember that everywhere you go, there you are. This matters in all of your interactions. You have to find peace in your own heart, head, and soul to be able to extend it to others. People who are highly judgmental toward themselves tend to carry that same critical lens outward. It becomes the way they see the world. Here's why:

1. INNER CRITIC = OUTER CRITIC

If someone has a harsh internal dialogue, they're more likely to project that same judgment onto others. It's not always conscious, but the standards they impose on themselves often extend to those around them.

2. MIRROR EFFECT

We often judge others by what we most struggle to accept in ourselves. For example, someone who feels inadequate may harshly judge others' mistakes to deflect attention from their fears or perceived flaws.

3. COMPASSION DEFICIT

When we lack self-compassion, it's harder to extend compassion to others. Judging ourselves makes grace and empathy feel foreign, so when others stumble or struggle, the response is often criticism instead of curiosity or care.

4. RIGIDITY AND CONTROL

Self-judgment can be rooted in perfectionism and a need for control. That same rigidity can lead someone to expect others to meet unrealistic expectations or behave in a certain way, resulting in frustration and judgment when they don't.

But here's the powerful flip side: The more grace we extend to ourselves, the more naturally it flows outward. Self-compassion softens judgment, increases empathy, and opens the door to more connected relationships. If you struggle with self-compassion, check out Dr. Kristin Neff's work, take her self-compassion quiz (https://self-compassion.org/), and learn ways to start practicing daily self-compassion. This work will change your life and create ripples of impact on everyone you have relationships with.

EXERCISE: PRACTICAL WAYS TO PRACTICE GENEROSITY

Here are a few strategies for incorporating generosity into your daily life:

- **Pause and reframe**: When someone's behavior frustrates you, ask yourself, *What might they be going through that I don't see?*

- **Offer space and grace**: Give people room to process their struggles without taking their actions personally.

- **Balance giving and boundaries**: Ensure your generosity comes from a place of choice and love, not obligation. How would your best self show up in this circumstance? Practice showing generosity even to those you might feel don't deserve it. Everyone deserves respect and dignity as a human being, despite what you may have convinced yourself. It's easy to justify, make excuses, and delude ourselves about our behaviors and focus on the other person's faults. This is a race to the bottom, and no one benefits when we take this route.

LIVE BIG OR STAY SMALL

If you don't get intentional about how you show up in your life, other people will do it for you. You'll say yes when you mean no. You'll keep the peace at the expense of your own needs. You'll stay in situations that don't feel right because you don't want to disappoint anyone.

When I was living by other people's scripts, I often said, "I had to." I had to show up, had to say yes, had to keep the peace, had to prove something, because that's what the script expected. But when I started focusing on boundaries, integrity, and generosity, I began to take back control. Those values became the tools I used to write my own script. And with that shift came a new language: *I choose to. I get to. I want to. I began to.* Language like that signals a new alignment. You know you're headed in the right direction when your choices reflect who you are and what matters most. That kind of life begins with strong boundaries, honest integrity, and a generous heart.

If you want a life that feels good inside—not just one that *looks* good on the outside—I encourage you to live BIG. No one is going to do this for you. The choice is yours and yours alone.

ANGIE'S ACTION STEP

Living BIG through boundaries, integrity, and generosity is a lifelong practice. Let's put it into action right now! Choose one of the following to complete today:

- **Set a boundary**: Identify one area in your life where you feel resentment or overwhelm. Take one concrete step today to set a boundary that protects your energy. This might mean saying "no" to something, having a direct conversation, or creating space for yourself.

- **Make a values-based decision**: Think about a decision you've been avoiding because it feels hard and scary. Instead of putting it off, take one small step toward addressing it and resolving it. Send the email, schedule the conversation, or write down your decision so you can commit to following through.

- **Practice generosity**: Choose one person in your life who could use some space and grace. Reach out with a kind message, offer support without judgment, or simply allow them to navigate their journey in their own way.

Living BIG helps you to show up in a way that aligns with who you truly are.

REFLECTION QUESTIONS: CREATING YOUR BIG LIFE

Take some time to explore the following prompts:

🦋 Write down three examples of times when you felt resentment or burnout. What boundaries could you have set in those situations?

🦋 Think of a recent decision you made. Did it align with your values, or did you make it out of fear or obligation?

🦋 Reflect on a time when someone showed you generosity. How did it impact you? How can you extend that same generosity to others?

CHAPTER 5

Redefining Success

I was born into poverty. My mother was just 16 when she had me. She was still a child herself and already carrying more trauma than most people experience in a lifetime. She had been raped and forced to have an abortion before I was born. I didn't know about that until I had my own son. But that revelation gave me a deeper understanding of the pain she had been carrying for years.

There was trauma in every direction—abuse from her siblings and step-siblings, violence from men, and a legacy of emotional wounds she passed down without language or healing. She coped the only way she knew how: through food, alcohol, drugs, and promiscuity. As a result, I grew up in a volatile environment where I didn't feel wanted. I didn't feel safe. I didn't feel like I belonged.

My father wasn't around for long after I was born. He remarried quickly and built a new family that I didn't feel fully part of. I existed in between my mom's chaos and my dad's new life. I was the kid who floated between homes but never really belonged in either. That fractured foundation left me with deep-rooted beliefs that I was not enough, not safe, and not worthy of belonging.

I now understand that what I experienced in childhood can be categorized and measured by a framework called ACEs—adverse childhood experiences. This is a widely recognized tool that measures the impact of early trauma on long-term health and behavior. There are 10 experiences listed in the ACEs questionnaire, and I experienced eight of them in my childhood.

Research shows that the higher your ACE score, the more likely you are to face challenges later in life like chronic illness, addiction, incarceration, or difficulty in relationships. In fact, a video called *Step Inside the Circle* powerfully illustrates how many incarcerated individuals carry high ACE scores.

My experiences and the resulting beliefs about not being enough shaped how I saw the world for decades. These beliefs distorted my relationships, opportunities, and my own sense of worth.

SEEKING SUCCESS FROM A PLACE OF SCARCITY

Unfortunately, those beliefs didn't stay in childhood. They followed me into adulthood, shaping the way I approached my success scripts. Believing I wasn't enough, I did what so many of us do: I tried to earn my value. I became a master at overcompensating by striving, proving, and achieving. If I could just check all the right boxes, maybe I'd finally feel like I belonged. Maybe I'd finally feel worthy.

My career wasn't a straight line; it was a wild river, winding, adaptive, and shaped by the terrain I navigated.

I've been a babysitter, Burger King cashier, a mill worker who stacks lumber, and a CNA who cares for the elderly and individuals with disabilities in home health settings. I styled clothes as an apparel stylist, served food as a waitress, and tracked heart rhythms as a telemetry clerk. I worked night shifts in a cleanroom as a photo operator at Micron, walked dogs, and cared for kids in my home as a daycare provider.

I've lived the layered experiences of being a military wife, divorcee, single mom, stepmom, and the family connector—the one who remembers birthdays, reaches out first, and tries to keep the ties strong. I've coached others as a personal trainer, spin instructor, and water aerobics coach. I guided young girls as a Girl Scout troop leader, finished a 70.3 Ironman triathlon, and captured life through the lens as a photographer.

I've stood at the surgical table as a certified surgical technologist, and later, at the front of a classroom as an assistant professor teaching surgical technology. I've served on boards of directors, directed a tutoring service, and facilitated growth as an educator, coach, and consultant.

Amidst all these roles, I also carried the identity of a lifelong learner. While working and raising children, I earned my bachelor's degree in workplace training and leadership and my master's degree in human resource development.

I've lived abroad as an expatriate in Shanghai, raised horses in the country, and most recently, stepped into the role of business owner, podcast host, and now author.

For a long time, I measured success the way we're often taught to. By checking the boxes. Get the degree. Land the job. Buy the house. Have the kids. Get the dog. Climb the ladder.

But chasing success on someone else's terms left me feeling empty. I was doing everything "right," and still, something was missing.

My ACEs had created in me a conviction that I wasn't enough. And when you believe you're not enough, it's easy to see life through a lens of scarcity. Scarcity of time, money, love, belonging, and space at the table. Success for me had become synonymous with the need to prove I was worthy through my various roles. It took rewriting this definition to break out of that not-enough mindset.

This chapter is about that shift. It's about moving from scarcity to abundance. I'll share what that transformation looked like in my own life and introduce you to someone who lives it out in an incredible way: my friend Jeet Kumar.

As you can see, I've checked a lot of boxes. But none of these titles alone defines me. Together with my hard-fought-for abundant mindset, they have shaped the lens through which I serve others. They are the roots of my leadership, the source of my grit, and the reason I believe deeply in human potential. They laid the groundwork for the calling I would eventually answer: co-founding Black River Performance Management and sharing the wisdom I have cultivated along the way from the experiences I have collected and connected on my journey.

FROM SCARCITY TO ABUNDANCE

A **scarcity mindset** starts with the belief that there's not enough time, money, success, or love to go around. It's that nagging fear that if someone else gets ahead, there's less left for you. This way of thinking gets reinforced constantly by the world around us. It keeps us comparing and competing instead of connecting.

For years, I didn't even realize I was living life through the lens of scarcity. I was like a goldfish that doesn't know it's *in* water until it's out of water. I grew up in a home where money was scarce and opportunities felt limited. That shaped my inner dialogue.

I believed I wasn't thin enough, smart enough, or worthy enough. And that narrative followed me into adulthood. It showed up at work, in friendships, and in my marriage. I became guarded. I armored up so I wouldn't be hurt. I downplayed others' wins because deep down, they felt like losses for me. The root cause was the belief that I wasn't enough and therefore wasn't safe.

WHAT IT FEELS LIKE TO BELIEVE YOU'RE NOT ENOUGH

Living with the belief that *you are not enough* is like trying to build a life on shifting sand. There's a constant undercurrent of fear, even when everything on the surface seems calm.

You might smile, achieve, perform, and give while silently second-guessing every word, every choice, every part of yourself.

This belief creates an emotional loop of insecurity. A persistent sense that something is wrong with you or missing from you. That you're too much, or not enough, or both at once. You may seek validation through approval, perfection, or overachievement, but nothing sticks. It's like trying to fill a cup with a hole in the bottom.

In *Atlas of the Heart*, Brene Brown describes "where we go when we compare." She notes that two emotions become prominent: envy and jealousy.

Envy is a feeling of wanting what someone else has, whether it's a material possession, a skill, or a relationship. It can be a benign emotion, motivating one to strive for something, or a negative emotion, leading to resentment and bitterness.

Jealousy, on the other hand, is rooted in the fear of losing something that is already valued. It often involves a third party who is perceived as a threat to the relationship. Jealousy can be a complex mixture of fear, anger, and sadness.

The core difference lies in the nature of the feeling. Envy is about wanting something, while jealousy is about fearing the loss of something.

They're both rooted in a belief that there's not enough to go around and that you (or your loved ones) won't be chosen.

When you believe you're not safe, the world becomes a threat. You stay hyper-alert, waiting for the next rejection, failure, or betrayal. You may not even recognize this as fear; it just feels like tightness in your chest, a weight in your gut, or a restlessness you can't shake. To me, it feels like constant low-level anxiety.

This isn't because you're broken. It's because you've been *wounded*. Likely by environments that made love conditional, safety uncertain, or identity fragmented. While this could be true in many ways, it could also be true that it was a way you perceived the event or circumstance that has kept you a prisoner in your own mind.

But here's the truth: These feelings are understandable and relevant, but they are not *facts*. They are echoes of a past that shaped you, but they do not have to define you.

Healing begins when you start telling yourself a new story: That you *are* enough. That you *are* safe. That your value is not up for debate. And that the awe, connection, and belonging you long for are not scarce. They are already within reach.

Scarcity isn't the truth. It's just a lens. A habit of thought.

The more I challenged that lens, the more I saw it as a mindset I could change. There is enough opportunity, enough space, and enough success for all of us. But I needed to shift how I looked at the world to start living like that was the truth.

THE JOURNEY OF JEET KUMAR

Jeet Kumar's story is one of the most powerful reminders that your mindset can either limit you or launch you. When I first met Jeet, he had just moved to the U.S. from India. No driver's license. No permanent job. He was working as a contract employee at Hewlett-Packard, navigating a new culture and doing whatever it took to get by. His early years in America were marked by scarcity, not just financially but in terms of confidence and opportunity.

But Jeet didn't stay there. He started investing in himself. Education. Personal development. Mentors. He searched for anything that could help him see beyond where he was. That mindset shift changed everything. His journey took him back to India, then back to the U.S. again, where he eventually launched his own company. What started as survival turned into success. Today, Jeet leads a multimillion-dollar business, creating opportunities not just for himself, but for everyone around him.

Watching Jeet's transformation gave me the push I didn't know I needed. During a pivotal moment in my own life, he encouraged me to attend a personal development program. It cracked something open in me, and I was able to see my scarcity mindset for what it was.

Jeet encouraged me to attend the next Landmark Forum in Salt Lake City and then set up follow-up coaching calls with him to share my experience. I was in the transition period of leaving higher education and becoming a full-time business owner, and my fear of leaving a "secure job" was holding me back.

I'm not sure how to explain the impact the forum had on my perspective. It is an ineffable experience that one must go through oneself. However, my follow-up coaching sessions with Jeet helped me navigate my uncertainty, fears, and threats (both real and perceived), as well as how my current beliefs were driving my actions. One of my biggest fears was letting a man have financial power over me. My history and wounds in this area were deeply based on the script that my Uncle John had expressed and projected onto me, as well as my lived experience up until this point in my life.

It took a lot of work for me to be willing to be vulnerable again, to trust, and to believe that money would not be a tool used to exert power over me in my new marriage. I had a lot of emotional baggage that I was carrying that didn't belong on this trip. Keeping that baggage would have been a form of self-sabotage, and I knew it. So, I went to work and sought outside help, ensuring I wasn't the one sabotaging my current relationships with an outdated map for my new journey.

Scarcity is often a script handed to you by your family, your upbringing, your environment. But just because it was handed to you doesn't mean you must keep reading from it. You can rewrite it.

REWRITING AN ABUNDANT SCRIPT

The shift from scarcity to abundance didn't happen overnight. It took real self-awareness and the guts to question beliefs I'd carried for years. The first step was noticing how scarcity was showing up in my life.

At work, I saw other people as competition. If they succeeded, it felt like I had failed. In my personal life, envy and insecurity would sneak in and make me question my worth. I wasn't proud of it, but I knew I needed to be honest about it to get around this obstacle.

I started asking myself some uncomfortable questions. *What am I afraid of? Why does someone else's success feel threatening? What do I actually want?*

Those questions opened the door to a whole new way of thinking. I started to see that abundance has nothing to do with how much you *have*. It's believing in possibilities. Abundance shows up when you stop seeing life as a zero-sum game. Someone else winning doesn't mean you're losing.

Gratitude helped me get there. I started each morning naming three things I was grateful for. The quiet cup of coffee to start my morning. The warm bed to sleep in each night. The kind text from a friend when I was having a bad day. That simple shift helped retrain my brain to focus on what was already working instead of what was missing.

And I paid close attention to who I was around. I made space for people like Jeet, who lives with an open heart. People who lead with generosity, courage, and possibility. That energy is contagious. And it reminded me that I could choose to live that way too.

TRAINING YOUR BRAIN TO SEE ABUNDANCE

Your brain is wired to notice what you focus on most. This is thanks to the **reticular activating system (RAS)**—a bundle of nerves at the base of your brainstem that acts as a filter for what you pay attention to. It's why, when you decide you want a certain car, you suddenly start seeing that car everywhere. Your RAS isn't creating more of what you're focusing on; it's simply highlighting what was already there.

When it comes to abundance, your RAS works the same way. If you focus on what you lack—time, money, opportunities—your brain will filter the world to reinforce that scarcity. You'll notice everything you don't have. But if you train your brain to focus on what you *do* have, the RAS will start highlighting the abundance already present in your life.

This shift begins with awareness and intention. One way to retrain your RAS is through gratitude. Start noticing and appreciating the good things around you, no matter how small. Write them down daily. This simple practice rewires your brain to filter for abundance instead of scarcity.

Your mind can be your biggest ally or your greatest saboteur. When you teach it to notice the "haves" instead of the "have-nots," abundance starts showing up everywhere.

REDEFINING SUCCESS

Redefining success was a crucial part of my transformation. I used to equate success with achievement—the house, the title, the recognition. I thought checking those boxes meant I was winning. But the more I grew, the more I realized success isn't about achievements. Success is how aligned your life is with what actually matters to you. Arthur Brooks is another one of my favorite social scientists, and his book *From Strength to Strength* helped me put language behind the scripts, roles, and understanding of the "hedonic treadmill" concept.

The hedonic treadmill is a metaphor for the human tendency to pursue one pleasure after another. That's because the surge of happiness that's felt after a positive event is likely to return to a steady personal baseline over time. There is strong evidence that some types of happiness are more durable than others. Pleasure that comes from doing selfless acts tends to outlast physical pleasure. Brooks also suggests that you can enhance your long-term well-being and happiness by practicing mindfulness, cultivating gratitude, pursuing personal growth, and investing in your relationships.

Harvard's study of adult development is the longest ever recorded. For more than 85 years, researchers have followed hundreds of people to learn what truly makes us happy and healthy. The number one factor is good relationships. Not success, not wealth, not fitness. People who had strong, supportive relationships lived longer, got sick less, and stayed mentally sharp into their 80s and beyond. Meanwhile, those who were stuck in a toxic relationship, lonely, and miserable saw their health decline much earlier. No matter how much money they made. The emotional connection protects both the body and the brain over time, and this, to me, is worth not only noticing but also practicing.

For me, success means forming deep relationships, engaging in meaningful work, and waking up with a sense of purpose.

ON MONEY AND SCARCITY

Since money is an area where many of us are conditioned into scarcity, I want to offer a perspective that changed the way I see it. I work with many nonprofit leaders who unknowingly operate from a scarcity mindset. They act as if the nonprofit *is* the mission, rather than simply the tax status. Many don't run their organizations like businesses and are often driven by high altruism and selflessness. These qualities, while admirable, can leave them overwhelmed and burned out if they are not aware of these strengths that can become overextensions.

The average tenure for a nonprofit executive director (ED) is around six years, though this varies by organization size, sector, and other factors. Annual turnover rates for EDs range from 18% to 22%, meaning many organizations face leadership transitions every 4 to 5 years. Recruitment for a new ED typically takes 7 to 10 months, and it can take over a year for that leader to be fully effective.

This level of turnover presents significant challenges, including the loss of institutional knowledge, disruptions in donor relationships, and decreased staff morale. Burnout, compensation issues, and the intensity of the role all contribute to these challenges. To mitigate these effects, organizations are encouraged to invest in leadership development, support systems, and proactive succession planning.

I've studied this phenomenon deeply over the past few years. In my search for answers, I came across *The Soul of Money* by Lynne Twist. She describes money not as a fixed resource but as a river with a dynamic flow of energy meant to move through our lives with purpose and intention.

When we treat money like a reservoir, we create stagnation, not only in our accounts but in our lives. But when we allow money to flow in and move out in alignment with our values, it becomes a source of nourishment, connection, and healing.

Twist writes that money becomes most powerful not when it's accumulated, but when it's consciously directed. Like water, it gives life when in motion. It becomes a tool for generosity, justice, and transformation. "Money flows through our lives like a current," she writes, "carrying our intention with it."

Money, then, is not something to worship, fear, or obsess over. It's a reflection of what we value.

When treated with reverence and responsibility, money becomes part of our service, our legacy, and our soul.

If this perspective feels foreign, I highly recommend reading Twist's book. Her life and work—spanning decades of nonprofit leadership, global fundraising, and co-founding the Pachamama Alliance— embody what it means to lead from abundance. She shows that money isn't something to chase or fear but to steward with intention. When we align our resources with our values, we create ripples of meaningful, sustainable impact.

She reminds nonprofit leaders that true wealth comes not from struggle, but from purpose, connection, and service.

HOW TO SHIFT FROM SCARCITY TO ABUNDANCE

Scarcity doesn't come from your bank account, your schedule, or your circumstances. It comes from fear, which comes from your brain. Our brains are wired for scarcity. Michael Easter's work in *Scarcity Brain* explores how our ancient brains are wired to crave more as a survival mechanism. This wiring made sense in environments of actual scarcity, but in our modern world of abundance, it often leads to overconsumption, anxiety, and disconnection. It leads to the fear of not having enough, not being sufficient, or missing out on what you think you *should* have by now. That fear is sneaky. It disguises itself as truth and convinces you that your limits are fixed.

In *Scarcity Brain,* Easter introduces the concept of the "scarcity loop" as a powerful cycle. The loop consists of opportunity, unpredictable rewards, and quick repeatability. Our evolutionary wiring drives us to seek out resources or rewards when they're available, especially when outcomes are uncertain and easy to access again and again. Whether it's social media scrolling, gambling, binge eating, or shopping, the scarcity loop explains why modern environments hijack our brains, keeping us stuck in cycles of excess and distraction.

When you're stuck in one of these loops, life feels like a constant competition. There's never enough money, time, love, or opportunity. But here's the wake-up call: most of that thinking isn't reality. It's a story your mind keeps repeating. And stories can be rewritten.

Start by noticing those thoughts, emotions, and actions (TEA) when they come up. When you catch yourself saying, "I can't afford this," reframe it to "How can I make this work?" That one shift takes you from stuck to solution focused.

You don't have to overhaul your mindset overnight. But if you start questioning those automatic, fear-based thoughts, you'll start turning obstacles into opportunities. And that's when everything starts to change.

Your life is a direct reflection of your unconscious mind. As Carl Jung put it, "Until you make the unconscious conscious, it will direct your life and you will call it fate."

ABUNDANCE STARTS WITH GRATITUDE

Abundance doesn't come from having more; it comes from appreciating what you already have. When you train your mind to focus on what's working, what's meaningful, and what's good, everything starts to shift. Gratitude is the tool that makes that possible.

Some people confuse this with toxic positivity. Gratitude is a practice. Toxic positivity is when we invalidate, minimize, or deny real emotions like fear, anger, or grief. Instead of allowing space for the full range of human feelings, toxic positivity pressures people into positivity, even in circumstances where other emotions are natural and necessary.

Gratitude pulls your focus away from what's missing and helps you see what's already supporting you. That shift alone can completely change how you experience your life.

Make gratitude a habit. Every evening, jot down three things you're grateful for. They don't have to be big. Some days it might just be a sunny afternoon, your friend making you laugh, or a song you love. What matters is that you're looking for what's going right in your life. I like to call this, looking for "AWE-pportunities."

This idea of AWE-pportunity rewires your brain and your default mode network to expect good things, to notice them, and to appreciate them. Gratitude is where abundance grows. It reminds you that you already have enough. And from that place, more good things can flow in.

The **default mode network (DMN)** is a group of brain regions that becomes active when we're not focused on the outside world and our mind is wandering, daydreaming, or reflecting inward.

While it plays an important role in helping us make sense of ourselves, an overactive DMN can keep us stuck in patterns of anxiety, comparison, and scarcity.

The good news? Practices like mindfulness, cultivating awe, movement, creativity, and even certain discomfort can quiet the DMN, bringing us back to the present moment, where peace, connection, and clarity live.

SURROUND YOURSELF WITH ABUNDANCE-MINDED PEOPLE

Spend time with people who see possibilities, not just problems. The ones who believe there's enough success, love, opportunity, and joy to go around. That mindset is powerful and it's contagious.

Watching Jeet shift from survival mode to building something expansive was a turning point for me. His belief in abundance challenged the way I saw my own life. Being around someone who operated from generosity, curiosity, and courage helped me realize how much of my thinking was still stuck in fear and scarcity.

Take a hard look at your circle. Who are the five people you spend the most time with? Are they lifting you up? Are they making you think bigger? Or are they keeping you small, even if they mean well? The people around you can reinforce your doubts or help you expand your vision.

Choose people who walk the talk. The ones who live in alignment, share freely, and support your growth without competition. When you spend time with abundance-minded people, your own mindset starts to shift, and everything around you shifts with it.

WHAT DOES SUCCESS MEAN TO YOU?

We live in a culture that shouts *more is better.* We look for more money, more status, more stuff. But chasing that kind of success can leave you burned out, disconnected, and constantly chasing the next thing. Real success? It's quieter. More grounded. It shows up when your life begins to reflect your values.

Take a moment to check in with yourself. What does success *really* mean to you? Is it a number in your bank account or is it feeling proud of how you show up for your family? Is it about being externally validated, or about doing work that matters to you?

Abundance and peace come when your actions match your priorities. How you spend your time, energy, and money aligns with what you care about most. That's when life starts to feel soul-filled. That's when success feels real and sustainable.

You don't need to chase what the world tells you matters. You get to decide. You can do hard things! It is scary and it is hard, but it is worth it, and so are you!

EXERCISE: MAKE THE SHIFT

Pick one area of your life where scarcity keeps showing up. Maybe it's money, time, opportunity, athletic ability, or self-worth. Write down the thought that plays on a loop in your head. Something like:

- I'll never get ahead financially.

- There's not enough time in the day to do what I want.

- I missed my chance to pursue my dream career.

- I am too old to learn to play an instrument, learn to surf, or learn a foreign language.

- It's too late to rebuild or rekindle a critical relationship.

- If I don't put my kid on this competitive sports team, they will be behind all their peers and will never have a chance at success.

Now challenge that thought. Ask yourself:

- Is this absolutely true or is it a fear/worry I've been rehearsing/ruminating over?

- What else might be true that I haven't considered?

- If I truly believed there was enough—enough time, enough money, enough possibility—what would I do today?

- If I weren't scared and money weren't an issue, what would I do?

Then take one small action that reflects that new belief.

For example:

- If your thought is *I'll never get ahead financially,* you might start setting aside $5 each week toward something meaningful to prove to yourself that ***I am open to attracting the resources I need.***

- If your thought is *There's not enough time in the day to do what I want,* you could block 15 minutes in your calendar each day for something that brings you energy instead of draining it. This will start to train your brain to see that ***I am open to prioritizing what matters most to me.***

- If your thought is *I missed my chance to pursue my dream career,* you might reach out to someone doing what you want to do and ask a curious question, just so you know ***I am open to exploring new opportunities.***

- If your thought is *I am too old to learn to play an instrument,* you might sign up for a free trial lesson or spend 10 minutes watching a beginner video to prove to yourself ***I am open to learning something new at any age.***

- If your thought is *It's too late to rekindle a critical relationship,* you could send a simple message to say you're thinking of them or share a memory to show yourself ***I am open to healing and connection.***

- If your thought is *If I don't put my kid in this sport, they will be behind all their peers and will never have a chance at success,* you might pause and ask your child what *they* want to try or enjoy most in order to model ***I am open to defining success in a way that honors my family, not fear.***

ANGIE'S ACTION STEP

Start a daily gratitude practice to shift your focus from scarcity to abundance. Each day, write down three things you're grateful for. Over time, this simple habit will train your brain to see what's present rather than what's missing, rewiring your perspective toward possibility and growth. Start today and watch how abundance begins to show up everywhere.

REFLECTION QUESTIONS:
SHIFTING FROM SCARCITY TO ABUNDANCE

Take a moment to reflect on the following prompts to help you un-cover areas where you can move from scarcity thinking to abundance:

🦋 What is one area of your life—whether it's time, money, rela-tionships, or opportunities—where you often feel there's *not enough*? What specific thoughts, fears, and actions (TEA) arise when you think about this area?

🦋 How might gratitude shift your perspective in this area? Write down three things you already have in your life that are sup-porting that area.

🦋 Imagine you were living with an abundant mindset in this area. What choices would you make differently? What would your actions reflect about your values?

Abundance begins with the way you see the world.

CHAPTER 6

The Power of Emotional Intelligence (EQ)

I first encountered the concept of **emotional intelligence (EQ)** while taking an online course. One of our assignments was to read *Emotional Intelligence* by Daniel Goleman and write a paper on it. As I read, something clicked. This was it! This was the missing piece for me, and I realized that many others weren't practicing this skill either.

I suddenly understood why some of the most intelligent people I knew struggled in relationships or at work, why surgeons I'd worked with could be brilliant but could not connect with their teams, and why some leaders inspired trust while others alienated those around them. EQ was the explanation for what I had been intuitively sensing for years.

Growing up in a household where I had to be highly attuned to the emotions of others, I developed a natural ability to read a room, pick up on subtle shifts in energy, and anticipate people's reactions for me to stay safe. While this had made me a skilled navigator of social situations and had become one of my superpowers, it had also turned me into a chronic people pleaser. Learning about EQ helped me see this tendency's strengths and limitations. It showed me that emotional intelligence wasn't just about understanding others, it was also about managing my own emotions, setting boundaries, and making choices that aligned with my values. It required not only knowing but also putting these tools into practice, even if it meant failing the first, second, or third time.

As I deepened my learning, I realized that intelligence and skill alone wouldn't determine success. How you handle yourself and interact with others is even more critical. That realization fueled my desire to bring EQ into my life and my work.

I was invited by a friend to participate in The Complete Leader Program and took my first-ever emotional intelligence (EQ) assessment. Something clicked. In that session, I approached our instructor, Ron Price, and asked how I could learn more and get certified to bring this back to my students, colleagues, and Technical Advisory Committee. I knew these were the *soft skills* the hospitals hiring our students wanted. Our college had always excelled at teaching technical skills and consistently achieved strong national certification results. But I was beginning to realize that while students were hired for their skills, they were often fired for their behaviors, most of which were rooted in low emotional intelligence.

One moment stands out. I had a student in surgery, passing a needle driver to a surgeon. The surgeon became upset that the suture wasn't loaded properly and, in response, threw the needle driver back at the student, causing a needle stick on his hand. It was a clear example of low EQ on the surgeon's part. But the student took it further. A 6-foot-5 young man, he ripped off his gown in a fit of rage and told the surgeon he'd be waiting for him in the parking lot.

His preceptor found me and recounted what had happened during what should have been a routine procedure. I then proceeded to have a difficult conversation with the student, and I wasn't sure how to even begin. I told him to go home and that I'd discuss next steps with our program director. He was ready to beat up that surgeon, and frankly, he could have. I listened to him. I validated his anger. I told him I didn't blame him for how he felt, but his actions had consequences that needed to be addressed.

In that moment, I saw my younger self in him. I knew that feeling of being wronged, humiliated, and wanting to retaliate. I grew up with the belief that you don't start fights, but if someone disrespects you, you make sure they never do it again. That was the language I learned. The default response.

This student didn't know any other way to handle the situation. His default mode network had taken over. He didn't yet have the skills or awareness that he had a choice. He reacted, instead of responding. And because I had done the same in my past, I could see it so clearly in him.

My program director and I both had empathy for him. We didn't excuse the behavior, but we understood it. We also knew the surgeon had put our student at serious risk. If the patient had carried any bloodborne pathogens, the consequences could have been life-changing. Thankfully, tests confirmed that the patient did not. But it was a serious incident, and we didn't take it lightly. We also advocated for the surgeon's behavior to be addressed but, as is often the case, surgeons who bring in money for hospitals are rarely held accountable for their outbursts, while staff and students face the consequences.

Stories like this fueled my deeper journey into emotional intelligence. Not just for my students but for myself, too.

What I found was that while many people were aware of emotional intelligence, very few understood how to apply it in their daily lives. And that's the only place where real change happens.

Emotional intelligence (EQ) is the ability to recognize, understand, and manage both your own emotions and the emotions of others. Psychologist Antonio Damasio's research has shown that emotions play a critical role in decision-making. He found that people who lack emotional awareness struggle to make even the simplest choices. This is because our emotions aren't just reactions. Our emotions are data. They provide valuable information about what we care about, what we need, and how we relate to the world around us.

EQ consists of several key components:

- **Self-awareness**: Recognizing your emotions as they arise and understanding how they impact your thoughts and behavior.

- **Self-regulation**: Managing your emotions in a way that allows you to respond thoughtfully instead of reacting impulsively.

- **Motivation**: Using your emotions to fuel perseverance, resilience, and goal achievement.

- **Social regulation**: Understanding and sharing the feelings of others, which leads to stronger relationships and better communication.

- **Social awareness**: Navigating interpersonal relationships with effectiveness and authenticity.

HOW EMOTIONAL INTELLIGENCE TRANSFORMED MY LIFE

Before I learned about EQ, I assumed that success was mostly about skills, intelligence, and hard work. However, once I started applying these principles, I saw a profound shift in both my personal and professional life.

I became more aware of my emotional triggers, better at handling conflict, and more intentional about how I showed up in relationships. I also started to see how much EQ mattered in leadership. People don't leave organizations because of the work. They leave because of toxic environments, poor leadership, and emotional disconnects.

HOW WE FEEL ABOUT OUR WORK MATTERS

Research from the Yale School of Management, led by Dr. Amy Wrzesniewski, found that even in roles considered low status, like hospital custodians, employees who saw themselves as part of the healing process felt more fulfilled and engaged. They weren't just cleaning rooms, they were caring for people. They crafted a sense of purpose within their role, even though the job description hadn't changed.

As Wayne Dyer said, "When you change the way you look at things, the things you look at change." That's the shift emotional intelligence makes possible. It transforms your inner landscape, which in turn changes how you experience the outer one.

Emotional intelligence shifts us from reaction to intention, from burnout to meaning, from just doing a job to living our purpose through it.

For me, the biggest challenge in developing emotional intelligence wasn't learning about it. It was *practicing* it. Knowing something intellectually is very different from applying it in high-stakes moments.

I had to unlearn some deeply ingrained habits, like people-pleasing, avoiding conflict, and reacting defensively when I felt criticized. But once I started making changes, I saw results almost instantly. My relationships improved, my confidence grew, and I felt like I was in the driver's seat of my life instead of riding along as a complaining passenger.

THE CHALLENGES OF DEVELOPING EMOTIONAL INTELLIGENCE

The first challenge I tackled on my EQ journey was unlearning the people-pleasing habits I had developed from childhood. Growing up in a household where I had to constantly read the emotions of those around me, I became highly attuned to managing other people's feelings. That skill helped me stay safe, but as an adult, it left me drained and disconnected from my own needs. I would suppress my emotions to avoid conflict, thinking it was the best way to maintain peace. But in reality, it kept me stuck in unhealthy patterns, saying yes when I meant no, and allowing resentment to build.

Another challenge was understanding my own triggers. I had to come to terms with the fact that my emotional reactions weren't caused by other people and were my responsibility. It's easy to want to control the world around you, to expect people to know how to treat you or say the right thing, but that's not reality. Life doesn't go according to our plans. People won't always meet your expectations (even reasonable ones like not trying to hurt or betray you).

I had to accept that if something triggered me, it was a signal that there was an area in me that still needed healing. Instead of blaming others, I learned to ask myself, *What is so upsetting about this to me? What story am I telling myself about this situation? What am I making this mean? What value is being challenged here?*

EXERCISE: THE TRIGGER JOURNAL

One of the most powerful tools for improving EQ is keeping a **trigger journal**. This simple practice helps you identify emotional patterns and develop more intentional responses.

1. **What was the situation?** Describe the event that triggered a strong emotional reaction.

2. **What was the trigger?** Identify the specific moment or words that caused the reaction.

3. **How did it affect my behavior?** Notice how your emotions influenced your actions.

4. **What would be a better response?** Reflect on how you could handle a similar situation in a way that aligns with your values the next time you are triggered.

This practice has helped me gain insight into my emotional patterns, allowing me to respond with intention rather than react out of old bad habits.

The hardest but most rewarding shift was realizing I had the power to choose my response in any situation. It's like Viktor Frankl's idea in *Man's Search for Meaning*: no matter what is happening externally, we always have a choice in how we react. He writes, "Between stimulus and response, there is a space. In that space is our power to choose our response. In our response lies our growth and our freedom." That concept was life-changing for me. It meant that even when I felt overwhelmed, frustrated, or hurt, I had the ability to pause, reflect, and decide how I wanted to respond instead of reacting impulsively. I never knew that was an option. That was not what had been modeled to me, but this space is where I began to find my power, my peace, and my freedom.

This work is ongoing. Through conscious practice, journaling about my triggers, and continually checking in with my values, I've been able to show up in a way that feels more aligned with who I am and who I want to be.

STAYING ALIGNED WITH MY VALUES THROUGH EQ

Emotional intelligence gave me the tools to recognize when I was out of alignment with my values. Before I understood EQ, I would react to situations based on habit, fear, or whatever emotion was running the show. I wasn't always intentional about how I responded, and that often meant I wasn't showing up in a way that reflected who I wanted to be.

Once I started learning about EQ, I realized that my emotions were signals telling me when I was out of integrity, when I needed to set a boundary, or when I was avoiding something hard. If I let resentment build, it usually meant I hadn't been honest about my needs. If I stayed quiet when I should have spoken up, I felt regret later. EQ helped me slow down and check in with myself: Am I acting from a place of courage? Am I showing kindness and generosity? Am I being true to what I say I value? Am I being generous?

Of course, I still mess up. I'm human. But now I can recognize when I've acted outside of my values and course-correct faster. That's the power of EQ.

The goal isn't to get it right every time; it's to have the awareness to adjust when you don't.

EXERCISE: NAME IT TO TAME IT

One of the biggest challenges in emotional intelligence is simply identifying what we're feeling. Most of us tend to operate within a limited emotional vocabulary—defaulting to "mad," "sad," or "happy"—without recognizing the full range of emotions underneath. But here's the thing: the more specific you can get about what you're feeling, the more power you have to manage it.

Tools to help you name it:

- **The feelings wheel**: A tool that helps you go beyond surface-level emotions. If you say you're "angry," are you actually frustrated? Resentful? Disrespected? Getting more granular helps you understand what's really going on. Just Google "Feelings Wheel" for options.

- **The How We Feel app (by the Yale Center for Emotional Intelligence)**: This app helps track emotions and recognize patterns over time. Many organizations use it to check in with teams before meetings, just like taking an emotional pulse check.

- **Body awareness**: Emotions don't just live in your mind. They show up in your body. Start noticing patterns. Does your stomach tighten when you're anxious? Do you get hot when you feel frustrated? Understanding your body's cues gives you an early warning system for your emotions.

WHY IT MATTERS

Naming emotions correctly isn't merely semantics. It changes how you process them. Psychologist Susan David refers to emotions like anger as *umbrella emotions*, meaning they often cover up something deeper, like disappointment, jealousy, or insecurity. The more precisely you can name what you're feeling, the better you can address it.

So next time you're feeling overwhelmed, pause and ask, *What am I actually feeling?* The simple act of naming it gives you the power to tame it.

BUILDING YOUR EMOTIONAL INTELLIGENCE

EQ isn't something you're born with or without. It's a skill. That means no matter where you start, you can improve your ability to manage emotions and navigate relationships. And let me tell you, this skill is a game changer. Just like learning to surf or learning to play pickleball, you don't show up as an expert on the first day. It takes time on the board or the court. You have to build competence to build confidence, and no one can do that for you. It's a practice you must be disciplined in.

After learning about emotional intelligence, I started paying attention to the people around me, the ones who thrived in leadership, relationships, and life in general. They all had one thing in common: they knew how to handle their emotions and the emotions of others skillfully. I noticed that the people who were good at it could sit with those in their darkest moments and listen, without trying to cheer them up or fix it.

EQ is something you build through practice, just like a muscle. Start by observing your own emotions without judgment. Ask yourself: *What am I feeling right now? What triggered this? How can I respond instead of react?* The more you do this, the stronger your EQ becomes—and the better you'll be at handling challenges with confidence and clarity.

YOUR EMOTIONS ARE DATA

Most of us were taught to suppress or ignore our emotions, push through, toughen up, get over it. But when you ignore your emotions, you ignore critical data that's trying to tell you something.

Your emotions aren't the enemy. They're information. They give you clues about what's working in your life and what's not.

Frustration might mean you're feeling unheard. Resentment could signal that a boundary has been crossed or most likely, never communicated clearly. Anxiety may be a sign that you're out of alignment with your values or that you have been triggered back into a scarcity mindset. Instead of dismissing these feelings, get curious about them. Ask, *What is this emotion trying to tell me?*

For me, learning this was huge. I used to think my emotions were something to control, push aside, or even worse, that they were a directive, something I had to act on immediately. Now, I see them as a way to understand when I need to adjust, speak up, or set a boundary. Once you shift your mindset to seeing emotions as data, you gain control and can use them as a guide to make better decisions.

It's important to understand that there are a variety of ways that **suppressed emotions** can show up in our lives and can be a form of self-sabotage. Oftentimes, we look to blame the world around us for our lack of ease, when really, we are our biggest obstacle and don't even realize it.

In Brianna Wiest's *101 Essays That Will Change the Way You Think*, Essay 56—titled "16 Ways Suppressed Emotions Are Appearing in Your Life"—explores how unacknowledged feelings can manifest in subtle yet impactful ways. Wiest emphasizes that suppressing emotions doesn't eliminate them; instead, they often surface through behaviors, thoughts, and physical sensations.

Here's a breakdown of the 16 ways suppressed emotions might show up in your life:

1. **Chronic anxiety or restlessness**: Persistent unease or nervous energy can be a sign of unprocessed emotions seeking an outlet.

2. **Overreacting to minor issues**: Disproportionate responses to small problems may indicate deeper, unresolved feelings.

3. **Avoidance of conflict**: Consistently steering clear of disagreements might stem from a fear of confronting underlying emotions.

4. **Perfectionism**: An incessant drive to be perfect can be a mechanism to control or mask emotional vulnerabilities.

5. **Procrastination**: Delaying tasks may be a way to avoid the emotional discomfort associated with them.

6. **People-pleasing tendencies**: Constantly seeking approval can be a strategy to suppress personal needs and emotions.

7. **Emotional numbness**: Feeling detached or indifferent might result from consistently pushing emotions aside.

8. **Physical ailments without clear cause**: Unexplained aches or illnesses can sometimes be linked to suppressed emotional stress.

9. **Difficulty concentrating**: Unprocessed emotions can occupy mental space, making focus challenging.

10. **Substance overuse**: Relying on alcohol, drugs, or food to cope may be an attempt to dull emotional pain.

11. **Overworking**: Immersing oneself in work can serve as a distraction from confronting emotions.

12. **Sleep disturbances**: Trouble sleeping might be due to unresolved emotional turmoil surfacing at night.

13. **Overcompensating in relationships**: Giving excessively in relationships can be a way to avoid facing personal emotional needs.

14. **Constant self-criticism**: An internal critical voice may reflect internalized, unacknowledged emotions.

15. **Isolation**: Withdrawing from others can be a defense mechanism to avoid emotional exposure.

16. **Persistent feelings of emptiness**: A chronic sense of void may indicate deeply buried emotions needing attention.

Recognizing these signs is a crucial step toward emotional awareness and healing. By acknowledging and processing suppressed emotions, you can work towards greater emotional well-being and personal growth.

If you want to change your life, start responding to it mindfully rather than reacting to it habitually.

RECOGNIZING VICTIMHOOD

When you understand and regulate your emotions, you're steering the boat. You stop letting the currents take you where they may. You stop reacting the way you've always reacted. You start choosing responses that align with your values and your goals.

Before I learned EQ, I spent a lot of time stuck in victimhood. I let fear, resentment, and stress dictate my decisions. But once I started practicing EQ skills, everything began to flow with more ease. I became intentional. I started responding instead of reacting. I leaned into the idea of *victorhood*.

VICTIMHOOD VS. VICTORHOOD

Victimhood (Stuck in the Wound)	Victorhood (Healing With Wisdom)
Replays the story over and over, looking for blame	Reflects on the story to find lessons, growth, or boundaries
Seeks sympathy or validation at the expense of action	Seeks understanding but also chooses an empowered response
Asks "Why is this happening *to* me?"	Asks "What can I learn or do *with* this?"
Avoids responsibility for current choices	Owns their response, even when not at fault for the event
Waits for others to change or apologize	Chooses healing even if the apology never comes
Identifies with the role: "I am a victim"	Acknowledges the event but doesn't become it: "That happened, but it doesn't define me"
Uses pain as protection or an excuse	Uses pain as a portal to purpose

It's important to note: Being a victor doesn't mean bypassing your feelings or rushing to forgive. It means owning your power even while grieving and hurting.

Being a victor is not about toxic positivity. It's about spiritual maturity: the ability to hold your wounds with tenderness while also choosing your next step with courage and living in accordance with your values, even when it's hard.

The phrase "every victim needs a villain" refers to a psychological and emotional pattern where, to validate one's pain or justify one's suffering, the mind assigns a clear antagonist. They need someone to blame, hate, or hold responsible. It simplifies a complex emotional experience into a binary: I am good. They are bad. I was hurt. They are the reason for all of my pain and suffering.

This narrative is incredibly human and often necessary at the beginning of the healing process. It allows us to name what happened, affirm that it wasn't okay, and locate the source of harm. In fact, acknowledging the "villain" may be a critical step in trauma recovery. But the problem comes when we stay there in that stagnant water for too long.

WHAT HAPPENS WHEN WE STAY IN THE VICTIM–VILLAIN LOOP?
Here's what I've noticed:

- The ego feeds on it. It enjoys the moral high ground, the clarity of black-and-white thinking, and the comfort of identity: "I'm the one who was wronged."

- The pain becomes a place of power. Instead of processing the hurt, we use it to gain sympathy, loyalty, or control over others, or over ourselves.

- It prevents integration. Healing requires complexity, compassion, and sometimes the painful truth that even the "villain" is human, too.

You can see this play out in real life when someone uses their children as pawns to punish another adult. For instance, a parent might withhold the kids from an ex-partner or grandparent when there's no real danger, or speak poorly about them to sway the children's perception. It may feel like justice, but it's really vengeance dressed up as protection. The victim becomes the one inflicting harm, and the ones who suffer most are often the children.

As long as someone is cast as the villain, we are locked into a story that limits our own freedom. We become prisoners of our own minds, caught in a loop where our healing is tied to someone else's punishment, apology, or transformation.

I saw this dynamic clearly during a transformative experience in a Mastermind Coaching Course with Peter Crone, also known as "The Mind Architect." His work helped me look beneath the surface of my reactions and pain to uncover the deeper beliefs I had been carrying for most of my life as lenses for viewing the world.

For me, those unconscious beliefs or constraints sounded like this: *I am not enough. I am not wanted. I am not safe. I am going to be in trouble for this.*

These were emotional blueprints formed through lived experience, etched into my nervous system, and reinforced over time. They shaped how I showed up in relationships, how I responded to criticism, how I sought validation, and how I tried to control my environment in order to feel okay. They were embedded in my default mode network, the unconscious mental programming that kept me in survival mode for far too long.

Peter has many quotes that continue to resonate deeply with me:

"Life will present you with people and circumstances to reveal where you are not free."

"People and circumstances don't cause your suffering, they reveal where you are not free."

"Every trigger is an opportunity to heal."

Those insights helped me reframe challenging moments to not feel like personal attacks, but invitations to heal. Every time I felt rejected, unseen, or misunderstood, it was revealing where those old beliefs were still swirling around under the surface.

Through the course, I began to loosen the grip of those internal constraints. I could choose presence over protection. Truth over assumption. Soul over survival.

If you want to rewrite your script, start by mastering your emotions. Learn to recognize them, understand them, and use them to guide your decisions. The more emotionally intelligent you become, the more power you have to see you are not defined by what has happened to you.

ANGIE'S ACTION STEP

Starting today, track your emotional reactions and suppressions for one week. Each time you feel a strong emotion, pause and name it. Ask yourself: *What triggered this? How is it influencing my response?* Each time you suppress an emotion, ask yourself: *Am I suppressing this emotion to avoid discomfort?* Write down your observations in a journal, a notebook, or use a notes app on your phone.

By the end of the week, review your patterns. Which emotions come up most often? What triggers them? In what ways do you suppress your feelings from the list above? What is your go-to strategy for suppressing these emotions? What would be a more skillful way to cope with these emotions? Use this insight to identify one specific strategy, such as deep breathing, reframing a situation, or setting a boundary, to respond with intention rather than react on autopilot.

Building emotional intelligence is a lifelong journey, but each moment of awareness is a step in the right direction.

REFLECTION QUESTIONS: STRENGTHENING YOUR EQ

Use the following prompts to reflect on your own EQ and identify areas for growth from two perspectives: your internal world (self-awareness) and your relational world (social awareness).

🦋 Think about a recent situation where you had a strong emotional reaction. What triggered it? Looking back, how could you have responded differently? How did others around you react?

🦋 How comfortable are you with difficult emotions like frustration, disappointment, or fear? Do you tend to suppress them, react impulsively, or use them as information? What do you notice in others when they feel these emotions?

🦋 Consider a relationship in your life that could benefit from more empathy. How can you practice compassion before reacting? Now flip it. Are there people in your life who practice empathy and compassion well?

🦋 Write a compassionate letter to the young version of you that believes you are not enough, not wanted, or not safe. I have even put a photo of myself at that age where I can see it to better write to this version of myself. What does that person need to hear? What truth can your soul offer in response? Then write a few lines of compassion to someone else who might be stuck in that same belief loop. What do they need to hear?

CHAPTER 7

Breaking Generational Cycles

On February 2, 2025, I passed the age my mom lived to. She was on this planet for 52 years and 41 days. Those numbers have never left me. When I hit 52 years and 41 days myself, I felt the weight of those numbers, but mostly I was struck by grief, reflection, and a little glimmer of clarity.

I wasn't just thinking about her death. I was thinking about my life, my choices, and the generational patterns that had shaped us both. I was grieving my mom while also carrying the responsibility of being the one who lived past where her story ended.

Here's what I now know with absolute certainty: trauma took her life. Her death certificate may not have said that in so many words. That's never the full story, is it? The full story was years of stress, silence, and self-sacrifice that would lead to an autoimmune disease. It was emotional pain that she never had the tools or support to heal.

And if I'm honest? I have seen those same signs in myself. I also have early symptoms of an autoimmune disorder that I am navigating. And that's forced me to take a hard look at the cycles I've inherited and the ones I refuse to pass down any longer.

In the wake of her death anniversary, this truth came into even greater focus when I listened to Dr. Sarah Szal on Mel Robbins's podcast. Dr. Szal laid it out plain: chronic emotional suppression, unresolved trauma, and burnout—especially in women—are directly tied to autoimmune disease. That conversation cracked something open in me. It was eye-opening. And it was heartbreaking.

My mom's story isn't unique. It is all of us. It's the women who were never taught to rest. Those who were told their worth comes from sacrifice. Who ignored their pain for so long that it became physical.

Eighty percent of autoimmune diseases occur in women. That's not a coincidence. That's a crisis.

And now, here I am, standing in a chapter my mom never reached. I have a choice. I can keep carrying the weight that broke her, or I can set it down and do things differently.

I'm choosing differently. I'm breaking the cycle. It ends with me. However, there will still be a legacy of trauma that I am not responsible for, that I was unaware of until the past couple of years.

THE LEGACY OF TRAUMA

In *Emotional Inheritance*, psychoanalyst Galit Atlas delves into the profound impact of intergenerational trauma, illustrating how the unprocessed experiences of our ancestors can manifest in our own lives. Through poignant case studies, Atlas reveals that individuals often carry emotional burdens, such as anxiety, guilt, or behavioral patterns, that are rooted not in their personal experiences but in the unresolved traumas of previous generations.

A significant portion of this exploration centers on the descendants of Holocaust survivors. Research led by Dr. Rachel Yehuda at Mount Sinai Hospital has provided compelling evidence that trauma can be biologically transmitted across generations. In a study involving 32 Jewish men and women who survived the Holocaust and their children, Yehuda's team discovered epigenetic changes, specifically in genes related to stress regulation, in the offspring. These alterations were absent in families without a history of Holocaust exposure, suggesting a direct link between the parents' traumatic experiences and the genetic makeup of their children.

These findings underscore the concept that trauma isn't solely a psychological phenomenon but can also leave a biological imprint, affecting descendants' stress responses and vulnerability to mental health disorders. Atlas emphasizes that this inherited trauma often operates unconsciously, influencing individuals' emotions and behaviors without their awareness. For instance, a person might experience chronic anxiety or a pervasive sense of fear without understanding its origins, which may trace back to ancestral experiences of persecution or loss.

Understanding the mechanisms of intergenerational trauma is crucial for breaking these cycles.

UNDERSTANDING GENERATIONAL CYCLES & THEIR IMPACT ON HEALTH

When stress and emotional suppression become a way of life, they can rewire our nervous system. Trauma changes how our bodies function, altering our immune response and increasing our vulnerability to disease. Studies show that chronic stress elevates inflammation, weakens our ability to fight illness, and even alters gene expression in ways that can be passed down to future generations through our epigenetics.

Epigenetics is the study of how your behaviors and environment can cause changes that affect the way your genes work, *without* changing the DNA sequence itself.

Think of your DNA as the hardware, and epigenetics as the software that tells it when, how, or if to run. These changes can turn genes "on" or "off," influencing how cells read those genes. What's powerful is that some of these changes can be passed down to future generations.

In *The Body Keeps the Score*, psychiatrist Bessel van der Kolk explores how trauma reshapes both the brain and body, often leaving lasting imprints that influence behavior, emotions, and physical health. He emphasizes that trauma isn't just a psychological issue but also a physiological one, affecting the body's systems and responses.

Van der Kolk explains that trauma activates the body's stress response system, particularly the amygdala, which he refers to as the brain's "smoke detector." This activation can lead to a state of hyperarousal, where individuals remain on constant alert for danger, even in safe environments. Simultaneously, the prefrontal cortex, responsible for rational thinking and decision-making, may become less active, impairing one's ability to assess situations accurately and respond appropriately.

Trauma can manifest physically in various ways, including chronic pain, gastrointestinal issues, and cardiovascular problems. Van der

Kolk notes that individuals with unresolved trauma may experience muscle tension, headaches, and other somatic symptoms without a clear medical cause. These physical symptoms are the body's way of expressing and coping with unresolved emotional pain.

The autonomic nervous system, which regulates involuntary bodily functions, plays a crucial role in how trauma is stored and expressed. Trauma can disrupt the balance between the sympathetic (fight or flight) and parasympathetic (rest and digest) systems, leading to symptoms like anxiety, depression, and dissociation. This imbalance can cause individuals to become stuck in a state of hyperarousal or hypoarousal, affecting their ability to engage fully in life.

Over time, this chronic state of stress can lead to chronic illnesses.

When I first started to make this connection, it felt overwhelming. I saw how deeply ingrained these patterns were in my family. My mother never had the chance to truly heal. And while I have spent years unlearning some of the unhealthy habits she passed onto me to cope with our legacy of trauma, the truth is I still battle them. I still catch myself putting others before my own well-being. I still overcompensate in my relationships, have difficulty concentrating, and work hard to avoid overusing substances. But the difference now is awareness. Awareness gives everyone a choice.

EXERCISE: TRIGGER YOUR OWN HEALING WITH GLIMMERS

Unlike the trigger journal mentioned in chapter 6, which focuses on identifying and managing negative emotional reactions, this practice helps you recognize the moments that spark healing. Deb Dana, in her book *Polyvagal Theory in Therapy,* calls these moments that spark joy in your day "glimmers."

By actively tracking what replenishes your energy, brings you peace, and fosters well-being, you can intentionally integrate more of those experiences into your life, especially in difficult times.

1. **What was the glimmer?** Describe the moment that brought you joy, peace, inspiration, or a sense of healing.

2. **What was the trigger?** Identify the specific thing that made you feel that way—a person, an action, an environment, a practice.

3. **How did it affect my mindset and well-being?** Notice how this positive trigger shifted your emotions, energy, and outlook.

4. **How can I bring more of this into my life?** Think about ways to intentionally incorporate this healing experience into your daily routine.

This exercise helps rewire your brain to notice life's glimmers rather than only focusing on what's wrong. The more you train your mind to seek out moments of peace and renewal, the more naturally you'll begin to build a life that supports your well-being.

TRANSFORMING RELATIONSHIPS AND HEALING THROUGH BOUNDARIES

Breaking generational cycles doesn't happen just because you *understand* them. You have to actively choose something different. You have to rewrite the script. And for me, that rewrite started with one thing: boundaries.

I'll say it again: Boundaries aren't walls. They are simply the bridge I put in place to help define where I end and someone else begins. They're how I protect my energy, my health, and my peace.

I used to think self-sacrifice was noble. It's not. It's a fast track to burnout and blaming others.

Do I still feel that old pull to say yes, to take it all on, to keep the peace? Absolutely. But now I pause and ask, *Is this serving me, or is it draining me?*

If I'm feeling resentful, exhausted, or on the edge of overwhelm, that's not something I can just brush off as stress. That's my body sending up a flare. And I've finally learned to listen.

LANGUAGE SHAPES REALITY

Maybe you too have caught yourself saying "yes" when you meant "no," just to keep the peace. Or maybe you've been stuck in the habit of saying "I have to," when what you really mean is "I get to." Those phrases might seem small, but they carry weight. Saying, "I have to cook dinner for my kids," sounds like a chore, but "I get to cook dinner for my kids" sounds like a treat.

If you want to shift how you feel, start by shifting how you speak. Replace "I have to do everything myself" with "I'm learning to ask for support." Swap "I should" with "I choose to." Try it for a week and notice how your energy changes. Real change can happen when you see yourself and your situation differently. And I have found that starts with the words I use.

ACCEPTANCE AND LETTING GO

I've learned that I can't change others, only myself. I used to think that if I just explained things clearly enough, if I just worked harder to show people a better way, they would change. But that's not how it works. People have to want to change. And if they don't, I get to decide how I want to move forward.

There are many relationships I've had to step away from as I have learned and grown. Letting go doesn't mean giving up on people; it means accepting them as they are while choosing to protect your own energy. Often, the hardest part isn't letting go of a person but letting go of the belief that things should have been different.

My mom didn't get the chance to break these cycles, but I do. I won't carry forward what isn't mine to hold. And if that means disappointing people who expect me to show up in the same old ways, so be it. My mental, emotional, physical, and spiritual health is more important than anyone's expectations or their validation.

SAFETYISM VS. PSYCHOLOGICAL SAFETY

In a world increasingly aware of trauma, there's a rising (and often misunderstood) desire to feel "safe."

Safetyism is the overprotection of ourselves or others from discomfort. It avoids hard truths, difficult conversations, or challenges in the name of emotional safety. While it can feel protective in the short term, safetyism often keeps us stuck in avoidance, disconnection, and fear.

Psychological safety, on the other hand, is the ability to be fully yourself without fear of punishment, rejection, or humiliation. It welcomes vulnerability, hard conversations, and discomfort as part of the process of healing and growth.

Here's some ways I explain the difference:

- Safetyism avoids the fire. Psychological safety builds resilience to walk through it.

- Safetyism says "Don't trigger me." Psychological safety says, "Let's explore what triggered me and why."

SIMPLE, FREE WAYS TO BREAK THE CYCLE OF DIS-EASE

I talk a lot about *dis*-ease because disease isn't just something that happens to the body. It's often the result of being out of alignment, stuck in survival mode, and disconnected from what your body actually needs.

Dis-ease is what happens when you override your limits, silence your emotions, and carry stress and busyness like a badge of honor. Over time, that dis-ease becomes inflammation, chronic pain, or autoimmune disorders.

If you want to heal generational cycles, you can't just do the emotional work. You must bring your body back into *ease*.

The good news? That kind of healing isn't complicated. It doesn't start with fancy programs or expensive solutions. The foundation is simple.

These basics are free. They're powerful. And they're how you break the cycle, not just in theory, but in your actual, physical body.

HYDRATION

Most people don't drink enough water, and yet, dehydration is one of the most overlooked causes of fatigue, brain fog, and inflammation. Your body is made up of about 60% water, and every function—digestion, circulation, detoxification—relies on it. Chronic stress depletes hydration levels, increasing the burden on your body.

Start with this: **Drink more water, more often.** Aim for half your body weight in ounces daily, and more if you consume caffeine or alcohol. Add electrolytes or a pinch of sea salt if you struggle with hydration balance. It's a simple shift, but over time, it improves digestion, energy levels, and even mental clarity.

NUTRITION

You don't need an expensive diet plan or a kitchen full of organic groceries to nourish yourself. Food is fuel, and every bite sends signals to your body, either promoting healing or increasing inflammation. Processed foods, excessive sugar, and alcohol fuel stress responses in the body, while whole, nutrient-dense foods help repair the damage caused by chronic stress. For example, I like wine, but wine doesn't like me. Every time I drink it, I regret it that night when I sleep poorly or wake up with a headache.

Start with this: **Add before you subtract.** Instead of focusing on restriction, think about adding more whole foods so that you get more fiber, more protein, and more healthy fats. Try starting your morning with protein instead of carbs to stabilize blood sugar and reduce cravings throughout the day. When you prioritize real food, there's naturally less room for the stuff that makes you feel like crap.

MOVEMENT

Exercise is about more than aesthetics, it's a commitment to health, longevity, and emotional and mental well-being. Movement is one of the most powerful ways to reduce stress hormones, lower inflammation, and boost mood. It doesn't have to be complicated. Walking, stretching, yoga, and even deep breathing all count as movement that regulates your nervous system.

Start with this: **Move daily, in a way you enjoy.** Walk for 10 minutes after meals to regulate blood sugar. Do a few minutes of stretching in the morning to wake up your body. If you hate traditional exercise, turn on your favorite song and dance. The key is consistency. Small amounts of movement add up over time.

REST

I love bed! Sleep is the body's time to repair, but it's often the first thing sacrificed in a busy life. Chronic stress disrupts sleep, keeping the nervous system on high alert. Poor sleep then fuels more stress, creating a vicious cycle that damages your immune system, mental clarity, and hormone balance.

Start with this: **Protect your sleep like your life depends on it, because it does.** Reduce screen time an hour before bed, set a consistent sleep schedule, and create a nighttime routine that signals your body it's time to rest. If you struggle with racing thoughts, try music, binaural beats, audio-guided meditations, journaling, or deep breathing before bed.

AWE-PPORTUNITIES

In chapter 5, I mentioned the idea of looking for "AWE-pportunities" or moments where awe can be found or created. Well, I'd like to bring it up again because awe is also a powerful healing modality. It opens the heart, quiets the ego, and brings the nervous system back into regulation. Awe makes space. It shifts our perspective and reminds us of what really matters.

The word *AWE-pportunity* first came into my vernacular during a private women's retreat in Avon, Colorado. We explored how awe can be intentionally practiced, not just stumbled upon. So, we began using the word as both a noun and a verb:

- **Noun**: a moment of wonder discovered or created through intentional presence

- **Verb**: the act of seeking or creating conditions where awe can emerge

I began noticing how awe softened stress, widened my perspective, and restored my sense of connection. It reminded me of who I was beneath the surface.

You don't need a mountaintop retreat to find an AWE-pportunity. You need to pause and be present. Awe can be found in sunlight shining through the trees, the belly laugh of a child, the quiet of early morning, the kindness of a stranger, or the memory of a loved one.

Healing doesn't happen overnight, but small, consistent choices like those I've listed above can create momentum. You don't need a perfect diet, an expensive gym membership, or an advanced wellness plan to take care of yourself. Hydrate, nourish your body, move regularly, get enough rest, and seek out awe daily. These foundational habits break the generational cycle of stress-induced illness and can create a new script for your health.

ANGIE'S ACTION STEP

Your health story isn't set in stone. You have the power to rewrite it. Start by reflecting on what you've inherited, both genetically and behaviorally, and decide what patterns end with you. Awareness is the first step in breaking generational cycles, but action is what transforms awareness into change. One of the most powerful tools for this process is the **trigger journal,** which you can find in chapter 6.

Each day, take note of what positively affects your well-being. What activities, environments, or interactions bring you a sense of peace, joy, or strength? Maybe it's the way you feel after a morning walk, a deep conversation with a trusted friend, or simply the act of setting a boundary. Recording these moments will create a personalized blueprint for what helps you regulate, recover, and rebuild. When stress or overwhelm strikes, you'll have a reminder of the simple, accessible things that restore your balance. You are not bound by the past, and you are not powerless in the present. I refuse to let stress, trauma, and self-neglect define my future the way it defined my mother's. And I hope, if you're reading this, that you'll refuse to let it define yours too.

REFLECTION QUESTIONS: BREAKING THE CYCLE

Take some time to explore the following prompts:

🦋 Reflect on the generational patterns you've observed in your family. What beliefs, habits, or stress responses have been passed down? Which of these do you want to break?

🦋 Think about your relationship with stress and self-care. Do you prioritize your well-being, or do you fall into patterns of self-sacrifice? What small changes can you make to better care for yourself?

🦋 Identify a time when you felt physically or emotionally drained. What factors contributed to it? What free or simple action—such as movement, hydration, or AWE-pportunities—could have helped you recover?

CHAPTER 8

The Power of Transitions

I've always been someone who moves through life at full speed. I've navigated major career shifts, personal losses, the ups and downs of parenting, and the evolution of my own roles and identities. For a long time, I thought I was just adapting to whatever came my way. I didn't realize that what I was actually doing was developing **transitional intelligence (TQ)**, or the ability to navigate uncertainty and move through life's changes with skill and resilience.

TQ is like EQ's overlooked sibling. Where emotional intelligence (EQ) helps us understand and regulate our emotions, TQ helps us understand the anatomy of change itself. Transitions are psychological processes instigated by the external shifts we experience in our lives. These shifts bring up emotions, challenge our identities, and test our resilience. As I've always said, you can't stop the waves, but you can learn to surf.

And yet, not every transition is about charging forward. Most times it's about allowing space for transformation like a chrysalis quietly reshaping a caterpillar into a butterfly. It's not just *How am I going to get through this?* but also, *Who am I going to be on the other side of this transition?* That's the deeper invitation of TQ: to see change not only as something to survive, but as a process that reshapes who we are becoming.

THE SHORES OF SOMETHING BIGGER

My husband, Rob, and I were wandering along the pristine beaches of Baja Sur, Mexico, with no agenda, just curiosity and conversation guiding our steps. We were dreaming aloud, as we often do, about what it might look like to host retreats in a place that felt sacred, nourishing, and expansive enough to hold transformation. A place that reflects the depth of the work we believe in, that nourishes the soul.

Then, as if drawn by some unseen current, we discovered something serendipitous.

A group of people had emerged from a nearby center, walking toward the shoreline. Each held a stick and began writing in the sand—words, symbols, perhaps intentions—watching as the waves rolled in to carry them away. The scene was quiet and reverent, suggesting this was something more meaningful than casual beach-going.

We learned from other visitors that this was Modern Elder Academy (MEA), founded by Chip Conley. When we looked it up, everything about MEA's mission resonated deeply: the commitment to purpose, the integration of life experience, and the honoring of major life transitions.

It felt like one of those discoveries you weren't actively seeking but somehow needed to find. The timing seemed significant, finding this place just as we were contemplating our own next chapter.

Our initial discovery led to deeper involvement with the MEA community through courses and experiences. I eventually pursued transitional intelligence (TQ) certification, which provided both language and practical frameworks for something I'd been experiencing throughout my life.

Now, I use these frameworks and practices alongside lived experience to help others navigate change with greater clarity and confidence. Whether someone is transitioning into a new career, stepping into leadership, or figuring out what's next in a major life shift, having practical guidance makes a difference.

Transitions are challenging, even when they represent positive change. They disrupt familiar patterns and can trigger uncertainty about our capabilities and place in the world. But developing skills for managing transitions effectively can transform how we approach life. Life itself is a series of transitions.

WHAT IS TQ?

At its core, **transitional intelligence (TQ)** is your ability to navigate change with awareness, adaptability, and skill. Just like IQ measures intelligence and EQ measures emotional awareness, TQ is about how well you move through life's inevitable changes. Transitions aren't just one-time events; they're continuous cycles of endings, the messy middle, and new beginnings.

MEA breaks transitions into three stages:

1. **The ending**: Letting go of what was and processing the emotions that come with it.

2. **The messy middle**: The uncertain, in-between phase where things feel unclear and you are "in the soup."

3. **The new beginning**: Embracing a fresh identity, perspective, or chapter.

Understanding these stages makes transitions more predictable, even if they still feel uncomfortable. And once you recognize where you are in the cycle, you can equip yourself with the right strategies to move through it with more ease.

LEARNING TQ THE HARD WAY

I didn't always have this framework. My early experiences with transitions were messy, chaotic, and like an emotional tidal wave. I wish I had known then what I know now. This is one of the reasons I am writing this book. My hope for you is that you learn the skills to navigate all the lifequakes life will present you.

One of the most confusing transitions I've ever gone through was learning to step back as a parent. When my kids reached their late teens and early 20s, I struggled to shift from being their full-time guide to respecting their independence. I offered too much advice. I tried to solve things they needed to figure out for themselves. My entire identity had been wrapped up in being a mom for so many years that I didn't know how to let go of being "Jakob or Alyx's mom." Honestly, for many years, that *was* who I was, how people introduced me, or recognized me. And I loved that role. It is my favorite role of my life.

The transition forced me to confront the fears and realities of not being needed, not being valued the way I wish to be, and no longer knowing my role or identity. It took time and tears, but as I began using and applying the new tools of TQ, I started to see it differently. I reframed my thinking: my kids' independence was proof I had done my job well. Instead of resisting the transition, I started focusing on what this new phase made possible, like rediscovering my own interests, deepening friendships, and embracing an evolving identity that's more about *who I am* than a role I played for over 20 years.

Compare that to how I handled starting my business and writing this book. Those were massive transitions too, but this time, I had the TQ framework to lean on. I approached them strategically. I recognized where I was in the transition process, acknowledged the messy middle instead of fighting it, and intentionally built new routines and support systems. The result? I'm moving through the uncertainty with more confidence, peace, and less self-imposed stress.

THE ROLE OF COMMUNITY IN TRANSITIONS

If there's one thing I've learned, it's this: You don't transition well in isolation. We need people—mentors, peers, friends, partners—to help us navigate the uncertainty of change.

When I was stepping into entrepreneurship, I surrounded myself with people who had done it before. I leaned on their guidance, learned from their mistakes, and borrowed their belief in me when mine wavered. When I became an empty nester, I found support in conversations with friends who had already walked that path. Community doesn't just offer advice, it offers *perspective*. It reminds us we're not alone, that we're not failing, and that transition isn't just the end of something, it's the beginning of something new.

PLANNING YOUR OWN TRANSITIONS

Successful and intentional companies create transition plans when navigating change. But for some reason, we don't do this for ourselves when we're facing major life shifts. Think of how we would benefit if we were this intentional in other areas of our lives as well!

Whether you're preparing for retirement, a career pivot, a personal transformation, or an inevitable life transition like kids leaving the nest, having a plan and a community makes all the difference.

A transition plan isn't about controlling every detail. Equip yourself with tools and strategies to move through change intentionally. If you know a transition is coming up, ask yourself these questions:

- **Where am I in the transition cycle?** (Ending, messy middle, or new beginning?)

- **What fears or emotions am I experiencing?** (Grief, anxiety, excitement?)

- **What support do I need?** (Who can guide me, encourage me, or offer wisdom?)

- **What rituals or practices will help me stay grounded?** (Journaling, meditation, prayer, movement, ceremonies?)

- **How can I reframe this transition as an opportunity?** (What is this making possible?)

By answering these questions, you shift from reacting to transitions to navigating them with purpose.

UNDERSTANDING THE THREE TYPES OF THREATS OF TRANSITIONS

When it comes to navigating change, our nervous system is wired to detect threats. But what we often don't realize is that not all threats are real, and many are shaped by past experiences, unhealed wounds, or old narratives we've carried for far too long.

To help people better understand this, MEA describes them as "triple threats." I take it one step further and describe these three threats as a lion, a tiger, and a bear because it can literally feel like you have encountered one or all of these three animals:

- **The lion** represents **you**—your inner critic, fears, and limiting beliefs. It is the voice inside that says, *You're not ready. You'll fail. You're too much, or not enough. You are not safe.*

- **The tiger** represents **your close relationships**—your family, friends, loved ones. These are the people whose approval you fear losing, or whose disapproval you dread.

- **The bear** represents **your larger environment**—your community, culture, workplace, or society. This is the voice of the world saying, *This is how you should be, look, lead, or live.*

Most of these "threats" are not physically dangerous. They are perceived threats. Meaning, they are emotional or social risks that trigger the same fear response in the brain as a real grizzly bear approaching you in Yellowstone National Park.

Let me give you an example:

Imagine someone who dreams of starting their own business. They feel the soul calling deep inside, but then the lion roars, *What if I fail? What if I'm not good enough? What if I'm rejected? What if I am not smart enough?*

Next, the tiger growls, *What will my family think? Will they support me? Will I disappoint someone by stepping away from the "safer" path they want for me?*

And then the bear grunts, *Will my community judge me? Will I be excommunicated? Will I get kicked out of the tribe? Will people take me seriously? What if I don't fit into the mold of success the world expects?*

Suddenly, their dream feels dangerous. Not because it is, but because it *feels* like a threat.

In truth, there may be no immediate danger. But the brain cannot always distinguish between a real lion and a mental one. That is why your awareness in this area is crucial for your decision-making process.

Learning to recognize the source of your fear is the first step in calming the nervous system and choosing a wiser, more courageous, and intentional response.

REGRETS IN TRANSITION

As with anything, the decisions you make in transition come with consequences, and these consequences exist whether you're choosing to act or choosing not to act. We might disappoint someone, lose an opportunity, face discomfort or criticism, or be left swimming in uncertainty.

But here's the truth: the regret of *not* doing the thing is often far heavier than the risk of doing it.

Daniel Pink's World Regret Survey, which gathered insights from people in over 100 countries, revealed that regrets fall into one of four core categories:

1. **Foundation regrets**: wishing we had made better choices to build a stable, secure life (like saving money or staying healthy).

2. **Boldness regrets**: wishing we had taken more chances, spoken up, stepped forward, or followed a dream.

3. **Moral regrets**: wishing we had done the right thing when we had the chance.

4. **Connection regrets**: wishing we had kept relationships alive, said what needed to be said, or reached out when it mattered most or before it was too late.

Of these, *boldness regrets* are often the most haunting because they come not from failure, but from silence and inaction.

Boldness regrets are born from the fear that keeps us from trying. From listening too closely to the lion, the tiger, or the bear. But regret is a predator of its own, and it hangs around much longer than fear does.

You can't always choose your transitions. But you can build skills to navigate them with more ease.

You can choose how you move through transitions, and that choice changes everything.

THE MENOPAUSE MIRROR

And that brings me to one of the most surprising, disorienting, and oddly transformative transitions of my life: menopause.

I wasn't prepared for it. Not emotionally, physically, or spiritually. No one warned me that this would be its own kind of initiation. This transition was marked not only by internal upheaval, but also by real, external changes in my body, my energy, and how I move through the world. Some days, I feel like a stranger in my own skin. Other days, I feel wiser, sharper, and more unapologetically myself than ever before.

What makes it even more challenging is that menopause has been historically understudied, underfunded, and misunderstood. For too long, women's health, especially in midlife, has been pushed aside or minimized. We're just now beginning to understand the profound hormonal, neurological, emotional, and spiritual impact of this transition. And so many women, like me, have had to navigate it in isolation, without adequate language, support, or care.

As Dr. Rachel Rubin, a leading voice in urology and women's sexual medicine, powerfully stated, "If a man's penis shriveled up at age 52, we'd probably have a vaccine for that."

That quote may make you laugh, but it also makes a sobering point. There is a double standard in how we treat and talk about aging in men versus women. The silence around menopause has been part of the problem, and I believe breaking that silence is part of the healing.

This transition has challenged my identity, my sleep, my memory, my relationships, and my emotions. There are moments of grief, moments of complete rage, and moments of profound surrender. And yet, it has also invited me to slow down, to listen differently, and to honor the cycles within me that are still trying to be heard.

Menopause, in many ways, has become a mirror. It has shown me where I still cling to youth, control, or certainty. And it has offered me a powerful reminder: You don't have to be who you were to become who you're meant to be.

UNDERSTANDING INTRINSIC AND EXTRINSIC TRANSITIONS

Inspired by Bruce Feiler's work in Life Is in the Transitions.

When we experience a significant shift in our lives, whether chosen or unexpected, we often feel like the ground beneath us is moving.

Bruce Feiler, in his deeply human and research-based book *Life Is in the Transitions*, calls these moments *life disruptors*. They are the large or small changes that force us to reorient, reevaluate, and often reimagine who we are.

Feiler categorizes these transitions into two types: **extrinsic** and **intrinsic**.

TRANSITIONAL INTELLIGENCE

INTRINSIC	EXTRINSIC
Changes that happen inside us	Changes that happen to us

• Shifting values or beliefs	• Loss of a job or loved one
• Redefining purpose	• End of a relationship
• A spiritual awakening	• A move or relocation
• Outgrowing an identity	• Major illness
• Questioning a path	• Starting a new role
• Feeling called toward something new	• Global or environmental events

EXTRINSIC TRANSITIONS: THE EVENTS THAT HAPPEN TO US

Extrinsic transitions are the external disruptors: events outside of us that shake up the course of our lives. These are the circumstances, the headlines, the sudden phone call, and the expected endings that still catch us off guard.

Examples of extrinsic transitions include:

- The loss of a loved one

- A divorce or breakup (that we didn't want or plan for)

- Getting laid off, fired, and starting a new job

- A new medical diagnosis (cancer, heart disease, menopause)

- A global event, such as a pandemic, political unrest, and chaos

- Children leaving the nest

- Natural disasters or accidents

These transitions often feel like our boat has been overturned into the river without warning. We didn't ask for it, we didn't plan it, but here we are, being carried by a current we didn't choose. It can be terrifying.

INTRINSIC TRANSITIONS: THE CHANGES THAT HAPPEN WITHIN US

Intrinsic transitions, on the other hand, are the internal disruptors: the quieter but no less powerful shifts that happen inside of us. These are the moments when something in our identity, beliefs, desires, or values begins to shift. Sometimes they're brought on by external events, but often, they simply arise as we grow, heal, and evolve.

Examples of intrinsic transitions include:

- Questioning your purpose or path

- Outgrowing an identity or role

- A spiritual awakening

- Shifting values or priorities

- Reevaluating relationships and choosing to leave an unhealthy or toxic relationship

- Realizing you've been living by someone else's definition of success

- The pull toward something more meaningful, even if you can't yet name it

These are the transitions that begin as a whisper or a longing. They are not as visible to others, but they can be just as disruptive and ultimately transformative.

THE BRIDGE BETWEEN THE TWO

Often, these transitions are intertwined. An extrinsic event like a layoff may trigger an intrinsic shift in identity. You might ask, who am I now if I am not this role I have been playing? An inner awakening may lead you to make an external change, like leaving a relationship or starting a completely new chapter.

The key is to recognize both. To honor the outer events that push us. And to trust the inner whispers that pull us.

When you understand the nature of your transition, whether it's extrinsic, intrinsic, or both, you can meet it with more compassion, clarity, and courage.

Life is a series of messy and uncomfortable transitions. And the power lies not in avoiding them, but in learning to navigate them with wisdom and grace.

EXERCISE: WHO AM I NOW?

Transitions change us. Whether triggered by an external shift (extrinsic) or a quiet internal awakening (intrinsic), change invites us to reevaluate our identity. In this exercise, you'll pause to reflect on who you are *now*, in this moment.

STEP 1: NAME YOUR TRANSITION

What transition are you currently experiencing (or have recently gone through)?

Is it intrinsic, extrinsic, or both?

Write one to two sentences describing the transition.

STEP 2: RECOGNIZE THE ENDING

What identity, role, or belief are you letting go of? What part of you feels like it's ending?

I am saying goodbye to . . .

STEP 3: ACKNOWLEDGE THE MESSY MIDDLE

What emotions or questions are surfacing right now? What feels uncertain or unformed?

Right now, I feel . . .

The biggest unknown is . . .

STEP 4: ENVISION THE NEW BEGINNING

What parts of yourself are being revealed or redefined? What strengths, values, or desires are becoming more important?

I am becoming someone who . . .

What matters most to me now is . . .

STEP 5: RECLAIM YOUR IDENTITY

Complete this sentence with boldness and compassion:

Right now, I may not have all the answers, but I know that I am . . .

The river doesn't cling to where it once flowed; it carves a new path forward and so must you.

WHEN YOUR BOAT GETS OVERTURNED

Sometimes transitions arrive as gentle shifts. Other times, they crash into your life without warning, demanding immediate response.

It was a beautiful fall evening on the Snake River, the kind of day where golden light makes everything feel sacred. I was enjoying a peaceful float with friends: calm water, low flows, and plans for a relaxing evening of connection and quiet beauty.

Our group included me, my husband, Rob, and two close friends. One friend was rowing for the first time on this particular stretch of river. While the Snake isn't known for dramatic rapids, its calm surface conceals powerful undercurrents and underwater obstacles from ancient lava flows.

As we approached our exit point, Rob offered guidance about navigating the tricky current near the pullout. I felt an intuitive nudge to suggest more caution, but I stayed quiet, not wanting to seem presumptuous.

What happened next unfolded in seconds. Focused on the destination ahead, our friend missed a massive, downed tree in our path or what boaters call a "strainer," a potentially deadly trap that allows water through but catches solid objects.

Our boat was pulled in. In that instant, I understood we were in serious danger.

The boat began taking on water. Rob shouted for everyone to get out. I found myself in the freezing river but managed to reach a concrete structure. One friend was clinging to branches while the other stood waist-deep in the current, holding our boat. Eventually, we were all able to get to some fallen trees where we waited for the professional rescue personnel to arrive and safely extract us from the water.

THE LESSONS I CARRY NOW

Once we were safe, the emotional impact hit—the what-ifs, the re-plays, the recognition of how quickly an ordinary day can become life-altering.

This experience taught me several crucial lessons: Trust your instincts, even when speaking up feels uncomfortable. Take safety precautions seriously, not casually. Recognize that surviving a crisis is only the first step and that processing the aftermath takes time. Understand that good intentions must be paired with competence and preparation.

Transitions aren't always gentle passages. Sometimes they arrive as sudden disruptions that demand everything you have. But if you're fortunate, you emerge changed, shaken, and completely awakened to what matters most.

ANGIE'S ACTION STEP

Take some time to think about a transition you're currently navigating or one you know is coming. Using the questions from the transition plan section, write down a strategy for how you'll move through it with intention, rather than resistance. Identify the fears you have, the support you need, and the opportunities this transition might create.

Transitions don't have to derail you. With the right mindset and tools, they can be the most powerful opportunities for growth in your life.

REFLECTION QUESTIONS: NAVIGATING CHANGE WITH INTENTION

Transitions can feel overwhelming, but developing **transitional intelligence (TQ)** helps you move through them with clarity and confidence. Take a moment to reflect on your own relationship with change using the prompts below:

🦋 Think about a recent or upcoming transition in your life. How do you feel about it? Are you excited, nervous, overwhelmed, or resistant?

🦋 Identify a past transition that felt difficult but ultimately led to growth. What did you learn from that experience? How can that lesson help you navigate future changes?

🦋 Who in your life has helped you through a transition? What kind of support was most valuable? How can you cultivate that kind of community moving forward?

🦋 Imagine yourself successfully moving through your current transition. What does that look like? What mindset shifts or actions will help you get there?

CHAPTER 9

From Ego to Soul

In the first half of life, many of us are driven by ego. But in the second half, something shifts. As Arthur Brooks shares in *From Strength to Strength*, happiness begins to hinge less on striving and more on meaning, connection, and spiritual depth.

Brooks describes this as a *second curve* in life, where our focus moves from performance to purpose. Spirituality, whether expressed through nature, faith, contemplation, or quiet knowing, becomes a critical part of this shift, offering clarity and peace beyond the titles and trophies we once placed above all else.

Dr. Lisa Miller, psychologist and author of *The Awakened Brain*, shows through decades of research that spirituality protects against depression, anxiety, and addiction while building resilience and a more profound sense of meaning. Her studies confirm that we are *wired* for spiritual connection and that people who engage in a spiritual life enjoy stronger mental health and a greater sense of hope and belonging.

Lisa Miller explains that while religion and spirituality can coexist, they are not the same.

- **Religion** is the structured, communal practice of beliefs, rituals, traditions, and sacred texts.

- **Spirituality** is the personal experience of connection to something greater than oneself.

Both religion and spirituality can be sources of healing and wholeness, and neither is required for the other to be meaningful.

MY CHURCH CHAPTER

There was a season in my life when I regularly attended a non-denominational church. It began during the early years of motherhood, when I was raising small children and searching for something deeper to anchor us and teach me how to parent with love and logic. I wanted them to grow up with a sense of spiritual foundation. A place where they felt safe, loved, and connected to something greater than themselves.

What started as an intention for them became something profoundly meaningful for me.

I joined Bible studies, taught Sunday school, and explored scripture, not from a place of fear or dogma, but from a place of curiosity and a longing to understand more. I was trying to find language for what I had already begun to feel inside: a quiet pull toward the meaning of life.

That chapter of my life gave me a sacred structure. It introduced me to community, rhythm, and the power of spiritual language. It also helped me understand who Jesus is and what he stands for. Through his presence, I never felt like I had to face my problems alone. That spiritual connection offered quiet strength and steady companionship.

Even in my scariest moments as a single parent, wondering how I would make ends meet, how to raise good humans in a chaotic world, or how to navigate a complicated relationship with a teenage daughter struggling with her mental health, and feeling the ache of my eldest son being away at college, I leaned on that connection. When things felt dark, uncertain, and lonely, I would often sit in the quiet and pray. I also sang out loud to God quite frequently, tears rolling down my face, praying for strength, guidance, and protection.

One of the songs that I would sing over and over again was Shawn McDonald's song "Rise" (2011), he declares:

Yes, I will rise out of these ashes, rise
From this trouble I have found
And this rubble on the ground
I will rise
'Cause He who is in me
Is greater than I will ever be and I will rise
Sometimes my heart is on the ground
And hope is nowhere to be found
And love is a figment I once knew
Yet I hold on to what I know is true
Yes, I will rise out of these ashes, rise
From this trouble I have found
And this rubble on the ground
I will rise

Today, whenever I play that song, tears stream down my face, knowing what I have risen time and time again in my life.

Three verses from the Bible became anchors for me in that season:

"Children are a heritage from the Lord, offspring a reward from him." (Psalm 127:3, NIV) This scripture reminds us that our children belong first to God. They are a gift, not a possession.

"'For I know the plans I have for you,' declares the Lord, 'plans to prosper you and not to harm you, plans to give you hope and a future.'"(Jeremiah 29:11, NIV). I have deep trust and faith that God is loving and wants the best for humanity.

And the story where Jesus meets the sick man at the pool of Bethesda continues to speak to me: "Do you want to get well? . . . Get up! Pick up your mat and walk." (John 5:6, 8, NIV)

That question. *Do you want to be well?* This was a challenge to me. It's easy to stay in victimhood. I knew it all too well. Many people I know stay in victimhood for their entire lives and never do their healing work. Healing is not passive. Jesus reminded the man (and me) that transformation requires participation. Sometimes, the first step is simply the willingness to get up. To take action, start the healing work, and stop having a pity party.

However, as much as I found comfort and growth during that time, I also began to feel a subtle disconnection, especially during my single years. Jesus speaks over and over again in scripture about caring for the poor, the widowed, the sick, and the outcast. His message is clear: we are called to love, not to judge.

And yet, in some of my most vulnerable moments, when I most needed community. I was more judged than supported. Not by everyone, but enough to feel the gap between the gospel and the actual culture. I kept asking myself, *Where is the heart of Jesus in these people?* I encountered many in the church who behaved more like the Pharisees and Sadducees, the people who frequently disappointed Jesus because of the way they misused their spiritual authority, prioritized appearances over transformation, and failed to embody the compassion and justice central to God's heart. They used religion as a weapon instead of a refuge.

Jesus' ministry was about inclusion, healing, and freeing people from shame, not trapping them in it. That dissonance and hypocrisy nudged me beyond institutional religion and deeper into a personal, soul-led spirituality: one rooted in the quiet certainty that God never turns away from the brokenhearted.

Spirituality and institutional religion are not always the same thing. My faith in God remained. My relationship with Jesus deepened. But my understanding of how and where I connect with the divine began to shift beyond the sanctuary walls.

CHOOSING PEACE OVER PRIDE

As I've grown older, I've felt a shift from ego to soul. I've come to see how much freedom comes from choosing stillness over striving.

A tool from Cindy Wigglesworth's *SQ21: The Twenty-One Skills of Spiritual Intelligence* has helped me navigate that shift. This is more than an Emotional Intelligence strategy because it is tied to a much deeper spiritual side of being. The tool is straightforward, and it's called SOUL:

SOUL is an acronym that can remind you to pause and what to do during that pause.

- **S**top
- **O**bserve
- **U**nderstand
- **L**isten

I use it in the space between stimulus and response. When triggered, I pause, and I use the SOUL framework. Doing so has helped me break old patterns, speak with more care, and protect what matters most. I still forget sometimes that I have this tool.

However, when I recall, I feel more at peace, have more clarity, and have less regret.

EXERCISE: DRAW YOUR RIVER

Take a blank page and draw a simple river flowing from top to bottom. This is the visual story of your journey from ego to soul.

At the top, represent where your journey began: the roles, goals, or identities that once defined you. Let the river twist, turn, or widen as it moves down the page to mark the various transitions, awakenings, and meaningful moments you've encountered throughout your journey. Add words, symbols, or names along the way that represent people, experiences, or spiritual practices that have deepened your connection to your soul.

At the bottom, let your river open into something vast and expansive. This is your soul-led life now, or what you're being invited into. Label it with a few words that reflect who you're becoming.

You don't have to explain this drawing to yourself or anyone else; let the river speak for itself.

A DREAM THAT SHIFTED EVERYTHING

A few days after our boating accident, and on the night of a solar eclipse, I had a dream unlike any I've ever experienced.

In it, I saw the entire world. Rivers flowing toward an ocean of love. Beneath the earth, dendritic roots pulsed with electric life, connecting everything. I saw the faces of people I've impacted, people who've shaped me, and even people I've struggled with. And in that dream, my perspective shifted. I saw every one of them through the lens of compassion.

Then I heard a voice say: *Love them, Angie. They are simple-minded. They know not what they do. It's your job to show them love and forgiveness. Bring light into the darkness.*

I woke up with tears streaming down my face. I shared the dream with Rob the moment he woke up. That dream changed something in me. It was like a sacred reminder: the ego may want to defend, deny, and dismiss, but the soul is here to love, forgive, and connect with people who are unhealed and hurting.

THE WISDOM OF THE SECOND HALF

One of the books that has deeply resonated with me during my journey from ego to soul is Richard Rohr's *Falling Upward*. In it, he describes how the second half of life is not just a continuation. Rohr explains that the first half of life is primarily about establishing identity, structure, and achieving success. But eventually, if we're willing, we're invited into something more profound.

Rohr calls this the journey of "falling upward", where the very things that break us open can also become the ground where our soul begins to rise. We stop clinging to control and certainty. We surrender to mystery. We begin to live more from our essence than our image.

This idea provided me with language to describe my own experience. So much of what once defined me began to feel too small for what my soul was asking. I was no longer trying to *prove* myself. I was trying to *im*prove myself and to remember myself, to live with humility, presence, and purpose. And to do that, I needed to slow down. Not to slow down to speed up. I needed to slow down. Period.

ANGIE'S ACTION STEP

This week, give yourself the gift of one intentional pause. Choose a moment when you're triggered by a comment, a delay, or a challenge, and practice the SOUL framework: Stop. Observe. Understand. Listen.

Notice what happens when you don't react from ego but respond from soul. Don't try to be perfect. Just be present. Even one shift can create a ripple of peace.

Want to take it deeper? Reflect in your journal: *What would my soul say in this situation?* Let your soul's voice, not the noisy ego, guide your next step.

REFLECTION QUESTIONS: GETTING SPIRITUAL

Take a few minutes of stillness today. Ask yourself these questions:

🦋   Where am I being invited to move from ego to soul?

🦋   Who in my life have I struggled to love, and what would it mean to see them through a lens of compassion?

🦋   What's one moment from my past where I've felt deeply connected to something greater than myself?

CONCLUSION

Writing Your Own Success Script

THE REST IS STILL UNWRITTEN

If there's one thing I want you to take from this book, it's this: your success script isn't fixed. It's not set in stone. It's not handed down with no option to revise. You are not stuck with what you were given. You're allowed—actually, *invited*—to rewrite it, every single day.

You are not limited by your past. You are not defined by other people's expectations. You are not too late, too broken, or too far gone.

Your script is *still unfolding*. And you hold the pen. (Cue "Unwritten" by Natasha Bedingfield, which just happens to be one of my favorite songs to play at high volume when I need a little bit of empowerment.)

Will there be fear? Absolutely. Will there be resistance? Of course. But you know what else will be there? Possibility. Power. Purpose.

Growth isn't supposed to be easy. If it were, everyone would do it. But the discomfort of change is the price of a meaningful life. You have to get uncomfortable to get free from the cage you have trapped yourself in. You hold the keys!

And every time you show up, get honest, and take ownership of your next chapter, you begin to clear the mental and emotional clutter that's been holding you back.

The river of life always carries silt and debris: emotional residue, false narratives, unfinished stories, mental clutter. If we don't pause to tend to these inner sediments, they build up, cloud our clarity, and weigh down our flow.

We all carry what Dr. Caroline Leaf calls "mental messes." Invitations to notice what needs attention, compassion, and healing.

You can go 40 days without food. Three days without water. Three minutes without air. But you can't go more than three seconds without thinking. Your mind never stops moving. And just like a river, if it isn't intentionally tended, it can get stuck, murky, or overrun. But when we learn to manage the toxic thoughts in our minds, we transform the flow.

Dr. Leaf's five-step Neurocycle program gives us a research-backed path to do just that:

1. **Gather awareness**: Notice your thoughts, emotions, and physical sensations without judgment. It's like stepping onto the riverbank and observing what's drifting by.

2. **Reflect**: Ask why. Where is this thought coming from? What is it trying to protect or reveal?

3. **Write**: Journal it out. Writing creates distance. It lets you hold the thought up to the light.

4. **Recheck**: Reframe. What's the real story? What can be composted, and what needs to be carried forward?

5. **Active reach**: Anchor your new thinking with action or affirmation—paddle to steer, ritual to return to, or a practice to protect your peace.

Dr. Leaf's research shows it takes 63 consecutive days to rewire a toxic thought and create a new neuropathway (far longer than the popular 21-day habit myth). So be gentle with yourself.

When you clear the riverbed, your deepest wisdom can flow.

RIPPLES OF IMPACT (ROI)

Chip Conley (creator of the Modern Elder Academy) popularized the term *ripples of impact,* and once I heard that phrase, I couldn't stop seeing the ripples everywhere.

People we've never met or barely know shape us in profound ways. A book. A single conversation. A passing piece of advice. These moments leave fingerprints on who we become.

Let me share some of mine. These are my pit crew, my personal board of directors, my mentors.

Years ago, I met Oprah while photographing at an annual conference in Sun Valley, Idaho, where she was one of the guests. Of course, she won't remember me, but I will never forget her. Her book, *What I Know for Sure,* shifted the way I think about clarity and intention. She made me believe that I didn't have to keep proving myself. I could live from a place of *knowing.* That's a ripple.

Brené Brown? She's my best friend who rides shotgun in the classroom that is my car, as I often have one of her audiobooks playing. Her work was introduced to me by my dean at the college where I was working. My dean saw a light in me that I was dimming, and gave me Brené's book, *Rising Strong,* with a card that had the quote by Anais Nin, "And the day came when the risk to remain tight in a bud was more painful than the risk it took to blossom." Since I love gifts and books, I took that as a sign, and I began to read every book by Brené, which gave me the language and a new vocabulary to name what I felt but couldn't explain. Vulnerability, courage, shame, and belonging are concepts I once avoided, but now guide how I lead, coach, parent, and write. More ripples.

Ron Price certified me in emotional intelligence, and that certification changed the direction of my entire career. I later interviewed him for a podcast episode on *Futuristic Thinking*, which just so happens to be a top leadership strength for both of us. What started in our class grew into a collaboration. That's what ripples do. They grow.

I read Shelly Paxton's book, *Soulbattical*, while Rob and I were on a sabbatical in 2024. I aligned so firmly with her insights and perspectives that I reached out to her and shared how much it impacted me. She responded within minutes! She inspired me to change my title to Chief Soul Officer and write myself a permission slip to live a more soul-filled life. The ripples just keep coming!

And sometimes, the biggest ripples come from people we never meet.

My surgical technology instructor once passed on a lesson from a surgeon she worked with. I've never met him, but his wisdom lives in my brain *daily*. (And those who know me, have heard it so many times they now recite it back to me.) This surgeon said that success in surgery and in life comes down to three things:

Timing. Positioning. Lubrication.

I call it the *TPL Framework*. Yes, it's memorable. Yes, it makes people laugh. But over the years, I have found it to be true in all aspects of life.

TPL shows up everywhere.

In the operating room, when seconds and precision matters (think: the timing of the surgery, the positioning of the patient, and the lubrication of the devices to enter body cavities), TPL saves lives.

In a tough conversation with your kid, waiting until they're ready makes all the difference.

In marriage, knowing when to speak and when to listen becomes its own form of relationship management.

In politics and religion, arguing too early or from the wrong angle only creates division.

When you're out on the open water in a boat, poor timing and off positioning can lead to real danger.

And yes, it even applies in the bedroom, which is probably why nobody forgets it.

It's a filter I now run almost everything through: *Is this the right time? Am I positioned well for this? Could I use a different approach? Am I bringing ease into this interaction or adding friction/resistance? Could I soften my tone and my pitch? Am I trying to control the outcome?*

That framework passed down through a surgeon I'll never meet has become a ripple that has helped me navigate life with more clarity, grace, and humor.

That's the power of ripple effects. You don't always know when you're creating them.

◎ You could be the person who says something in a meeting that changes the direction of someone else's career.

- ◎ You could be the one to give a book or send a podcast to someone that you believe in and watch them transform.

- ◎ You could model boundary-setting in a way that gives your daughter permission to do the same.

- ◎ You could model boundary-setting with your spouse that gives your son a clear message on how he will treat his future partner.

- ◎ You could create the space for a life-saving conversation when someone is in a downward spiral and considering taking their own life.

- ◎ You could share your story and unknowingly give someone else the courage to rewrite theirs.

So if you're sitting here thinking, *Who am I to change the script?* that is your ego, and sometimes your ego is not your amigo! So let me answer that for you right now.

If not you, then who? You're someone with ripples already in motion.

REWRITING NEVER ENDS

Rewriting isn't a one-time choice. It's a practice. And some days, it will feel like two strokes forward, one stroke back. You'll doubt. You'll question. You'll want to retreat into old patterns. That's normal. That's human.

With every new chapter, you get a chance to realign. With every job change, heartbreak, relocation, reunion, diagnosis, and break-through, you get to let go of the pages that no longer serve you and write new ones that actually reflect who you *are*.

I know this because I'm still doing it. I've rewritten my script through grief, career shifts, motherhood, entrepreneurship, and self-discovery. And even now as I type these words, I know I'm not done. I'm in the messy middle of it. Just like you. Something I know for sure is this: your worst chapter is not your last chapter.

YOUR NEXT STEP STARTS NOW

You've read the book. You've resonated with the stories I've shared. You've started to see your own patterns.

Now it's time to act.

You can't heal what you won't face. That thing that you don't want to share is where your true power is. Your wounds contain your wisdom. Shame cannot exist in the spotlight.

What's one part of your script you're ready to rewrite?

Maybe it's forgiving yourself so you can forgive others.

Maybe it's how you talk to yourself.

Maybe it's how you show up in relationships.

Maybe it's how you lead, how you rest, or how you ask for what you need.

And if you want support, I'm here. I work with individuals and teams who are ready to get intentional about change. Whether it's through coaching, workshops, or corporate training, I help people develop the EQ, TQ, and mindset they need to navigate life with clarity and courage. You are valuable and worthy of investment and once you know that, you will be unstoppable.

Because this isn't just about personal or professional growth. This is about legacy . . . about ripples . . . about impact that lasts and a life that is meaningful to you.

So go write your next chapter. Go break the cycle. Go live the script that *actually belongs to you.*

Emerge.

Acknowledgments

TO THE ONE WHO HAS ALWAYS WALKED WITH ME—

Even when I felt alone, I never truly was.

Through every transition, synchronicity, serendipity, heartbreak, opportunity, and unknown—there was always something greater holding me. Guiding me. Nudging me forward when I couldn't see the way.

I don't speak of religion, but of relationship.

Not doctrine, but divine direction.

A quiet presence that showed up through sunsets, strangers, songs on the radio, gut feelings, and grace I didn't earn but received anyway.

To the Universe, to Jesus, to the sacred rhythm that has woven beauty from my brokenness—thank you. You have been the guide of my soul's journey.

My protector, my provider, and the whisper that reminded me: *you are not lost, just becoming.*

I owe every wave, every step, and every rising to You.

TO THE SPIRITUAL GUIDES WHO ILLUMINATED THE PATH—

To Pastor Jason & Janet Cahill, thank you. Your love, faith, and spiritual leadership helped me see that I could be both strong and soft, grounded and growing.

To Shaman Saul, your wisdom has opened doors to deeper healing and connection to the sacred. You helped me reclaim parts of myself I didn't even know I had lost.

To my MEA family, and more specifically to Joelle, Kristine, and Leslie, your hands have been extensions of grace. Through your healing work, you offered not only relief, but remembrance—that my body is worthy of care, my spirit is deserving of rest, and that going back into the womb for healing is sacred work. I am held, I am loved, I am connected to source.

To those whose teachings found me at just the right time—Eckhart Tolle, Deepak Chopra, Richard Rohr, Oprah, Mother Teresa, Mahatma Gandhi, Paulo Coelho, Don Miguel Ruiz, Lynne Twist, and Jeet Kumar—thank you for showing me the power of presence, compassion, courage, and abundance. You taught me that leadership begins with service, that truth liberates, that generosity transforms, and that the quietest acts of love often leave the deepest impact.

Your words have been my mirrors.

Your work, a thread in the spiritual fabric of this book.

TO THE ONES WHO HELPED ME STEP INTO THE CURRENT—

Jeff Hamoui and Dacher Keltner—thank you for seeing what I couldn't yet see. You challenged the voice in my head that kept asking, *Who am I to write a book?* and reminded me instead to ask,

Who might be helped if I do? Your encouragement helped me shift from ego to purpose, from doubt to service. That nudge stirred something deep within me—the call to write, to share, to give my story away.

Rob—my love, my counterpartner, my business partner, my confidant, my best friend, my raison d'être—your steady support, patience, and belief in me made this possible. You held space for me and have always seen me and helped me to reach my potential.

To Aloha Publishing—thank you for walking alongside me with clarity, kindness, and heart. Your team's support turned possibility into reality, and I'm deeply grateful.

And to Jeremy Graves—your belief in my voice, your invitation to speak, and your generous connection to Aloha lit the path forward. You helped me say yes to myself.

TO THE GIRL I ONCE WAS—

I am so damn proud of you!

The cards you were dealt didn't set you up for success, but you played the hell out of those cards. You could have stayed in victimhood, blaming others for the pain you didn't deserve—but you didn't. You chose a different path. You became a cycle-breaker, a change agent in our family, turning pain into purpose.

You didn't get it perfect—but you never gave up. You are a riser! You are an overcomer! You are learning to stay curious instead of defensive. To soften without shrinking. To pause before reacting. You no longer strive to be right—you strive to get it right. And that shift is one of your greatest teachers.

In your short time on this planet, you have *mastered forgiveness and resilience* at the Ph.D. level. You've learned to let go without forgetting, to heal without hardening. And while there is still more river to travel, you are flowing with more grace, more strength, and more soul than ever before.

You are a beautiful soul.

Worthy of love, kindness, generosity, and peace.

Still growing. Still healing. Still emerging.

And to every reader on their own path to *emerging into their authentic self—*

You are not behind. You are not broken.

You are in the river of life, learning to trust the flow. Keep going.

TO MY ROOTS—

To my mom, Paula—you gave me life and a love for water that has always been my refuge. Some of my earliest memories of joy and freedom trace back to swimming in rivers and lakes by your side. Our journey wasn't always easy, and there were times I longed for more of you. But I've come to understand that you showed your love the best way you knew how—through your hands, through your heart. You cooked, you sewed, and you created keepsakes for me and for my children, your grandchildren. For the short time they had with you, I know they felt your warmth and your giving spirit. You were one of the most generous people I've ever known—with very little to give by the world's standards, yet you gave everything you had. And now, as I age, I see you when I look in the mirror.

In my reflection, I carry your story.

In my becoming, I carry your strength, your tender heart, and your weepy baby blues. I love you.

To my dad, Patrick—you gave me the gift of music, and with it, a portal to awe. I loved watching you play the drums and sing with such raw, unfiltered joy. You were self-taught and deeply talented, and through you, I learned that music wasn't just sound—it was soul. I carry that rhythm in me still. I may not play an instrument (yet), but I can name that tune, recall lyrics tucked deep in memory, and bring the house down at karaoke—just like you. Some of our deepest conversations happened around a campfire. I have your hands and your skinny ankles. Your electric blue eyes. And your humor—sharp, disarming, and unforgettable. Our relationship wasn't always as fulfilling as I needed as a little girl, but I carry the best of you forward, and I love you.

To my Aunt Babe—my GREAT aunt. You loved me as if I were your own. You made me feel safe, seen, and wholly loved. I know I wouldn't be where I am today without your selflessness. You gave your time, your money, your heart, your hope and generosity for children that were not your responsibility. You created ripples of impact that have no end. You sang to me—"When Irish Eyes Are Smiling" and "You Are My Sunshine"—songs that still echo in my soul. You introduced me to tradition, to family legacy, to Palouse and Sunday dinners, to dressing up for Easter, and never leaving the house without lipstick. You and Grandma Berniece gave me countless matching outfits with cousin Jenny, and in those moments, I felt beautiful and cherished. You showed me awe through *moral beauty*—and you *are* moral beauty. With Uncle John's belief in education as my way out, I built the foundation that carried me forward just as he knew it would. I carry you with me, always.

To Susan & Bob—thank you for the countless memories and experiences on the Aft Cabin Barracuda on my favorite lake that you made possible for me, my kids, and even my friends. Thank you for showing up for me when I needed help, grace, perspective, and love. Thank you for modeling resilience through life's hardest transitions and for allowing me to witness your love and the kidney transplant that Bob so graciously gave to Susan to extend her life. I am still in awe of the moral beauty of that experience.

To my grandparents—thank you for your resilience. Even without the tools to heal, you passed down strength I now honor. I carry your stories, your sacrifices, and your songs in my bones. From home-cooked meals and pies to homebrews to tending gardens, I felt your love and grace towards this unexpected child thrust into your family much earlier than you had hoped for.

To my siblings—Andrew, Michelle, and Kristie—we came through the same river, though the currents pulled us in different ways. I love you deeply. No matter how far we drift, the water that connects us will always run through me. Thank you for your consistent love and support.

To my cousins—thank you for being the joy in the chaos, the laughter in the dysfunction, and the resilience wrapped in wit and a smart mouth. We may have grown up in wild, unpredictable waters, but you helped me find the fun in the flood. Our shared stories—equal parts survival and sharp comebacks—taught me how to bend without breaking. I carry that strength and those smiles with me always.

And to my nieces and nephews, each of you holds a piece of our family story. Watching you grow and step into your own truths brings me endless joy. You are the next wave, and I am cheering you on with my whole heart. I am happy to be a guide when life gets hard. Reach out and ask for help when you are ready. I am happy to share my wisdom with you and reassure you that you can do hard things.

TO MY FUTURE—

To my children, Jakob and Alyx—you are my greatest teachers, my deepest joy, and the reason I keep rising. Becoming your mom changed the course of my life. You gave me purpose in my pain, light in my darkness, and fuel for my healing. I didn't always get it right, but I always tried to grow and be better for you. You've witnessed my becoming, and I hope in doing so, you've found the courage for your own healing and growth.

Jakob, watching you grow into the man you are and the father you are becoming, fills me with awe. I love your intuitive and sensitive soul, your quiet strength, and the way you move through the world with depth and compassion. You are magnetic, incredibly musically gifted, and your creativity is a language all its own. Your daughter is lucky to have you as her guide, just as I've been lucky to walk beside you as your mom. You have always had a rhythm all your own, and the world needs your music, your heart, and your presence. Every little girl and boy deserves a father like you.

Alyx, your passion, your brilliance, your heart, and your feistiness— I see so much of myself in you, and so much that is entirely your own. You have a fire that refuses to be dimmed and a wisdom beyond your years. Your ability to speak truth with conviction and love is a gift to everyone around you. And your athleticism—my goodness, it amazes me. Whether you were dominating on a court, lighting up a softball field, or pushing yourself in the gym, I've watched in awe as your body and spirit move with determination. You are fierce and kind, strong and soft, thoughtful and driven. I am endlessly proud of the woman you are and the legacy of love, courage, and resilience you're creating.

To Aubrey—thank you for loving my son, for being his partner in life, and for welcoming me into your journey. Your grace, your openness, and the way you mother our sweet girl are gifts I don't take for granted. I see the strength in your quiet moments, the love in your gentle presence, and the beauty in the life you're building together. You have brought warmth and stability to Jakob's world, and watching the two of you parent with care, laughter, and intention fills me with such peace. Thank you for letting me be part of your story—for allowing me to step into the role of Gigi with joy and gratitude. Our little Mavy is so lucky to have you as her mom. So am I.

And to Mavis ("Mavy")—my granddaughter, my little angel, my sunshine, my soul's reminder of what matters most. You are the continuation of a story I prayed would feel softer and safer than the one I began in. You are joy embodied. May you always know how deeply you are loved, and may this book be part of the legacy I leave for you: one of healing, hope, and rising with the river.

To Ian and Leland—being your bonus mom has been one of the greatest honors of my life. I didn't give you life, but life gave me you—and for that, I'm grateful. Watching you grow into such strong, thoughtful men fills me with pride. Thank you for letting me be part of your journey.

THE MENTORS WHO SHAPED MY BECOMING—

To the mentors who have walked beside me and poured into my growth with generosity and truth—Mona, Dinu, Cathleen, Ron, Jeet, and Rob—thank you. You have challenged me, championed me, and reminded me of who I am when I forget. I carry your wisdom like stones in my pocket—grounding me when the current runs fast.

To Chip Conley, founder of the Modern Elder Academy and mentor not only to Rob and me, but to thousands of MEA alumni—your ripples of impact are beyond what you'll ever fully know. You are the real deal. You see us, not for our lacking titles or limited status, but for who we are as humans and souls. You acknowledge, encourage, and uplift, even when no one's watching. You walk the walk. Your grounded wisdom, generous heart, and soulful leadership have shaped our lives in ways that words can only begin to honor.

And to the mentors who don't know me—but have influenced me in ways that words can barely hold—Brené Brown, you're one of my best friends (you just don't know it yet).

Oprah, I photographed you multiple times at an annual billionaire conference in Sun Valley, Idaho—some images were printed and framed on the wall, some were sent home with you in an Italian leather frame, and others made their way into a photo album that you received at Christmas time. I loved your energy. Being in your and Gayle's peaceful presence was something I could *feel*—steady, grounded, magnetic. But I wasn't allowed to speak to you. I was only "the help" at the conference. And still . . . you left a lasting impression and ripples of impact.

Adam Grant, thank you for helping me learn to think again—and again—and giving me permission to change my mind when I got new data. And for giving me the awareness to shift me from being a taker to a conscious giver or, at the very least, a matcher.

Arthur Brooks, for illuminating the difference between fluid and crystallized intelligence and teaching me how to build a life anchored in meaning, not just success.

And to my emotional intelligence giants—Daniel Goleman, Travis Bradberry, Susan David, Marc Brackett, and Dacher Keltner—thank you for shaping the work that's now shaping others.

Robert Waldinger and everyone involved in the world's longest study on What Makes A Good Life, for sharing it on a TED Talk.

You've each influenced the pages of this book in your own way. Your ideas have rippled through my river, and I'm so grateful.

TO MY CHOSEN FAMILY—MY FRIENDS—

To Chrystie, Conra, Laurie, Kelli, Michelle, Mona, Karri, Sarah, Cherisse, Shantay, Tiffani, Ali, Rachael, Brandy & Brett, Jeff, Joelle, Leslie, and Christine—thank you.

Some of you have been with me for most of my life, witnessing all the messy, miraculous, in-between parts of my journey. Others arrived more recently—exactly when I needed you, as if the universe placed you at the river's bend to help guide me forward.

You've held space for my evolution. You've cheered for my growth, poured into my healing, and loved me through the murky and the clear. You've shown up with laughter, honesty, grace, and generosity—and I don't take that lightly.

Friends are the family we get to choose. I choose you—again and again—because of the way you show up with love and light. Thank you for walking with me. I wouldn't want to do this life without you.

TO MY FELLOW CYCLE-BREAKERS—

I see you.

The ones who are doing the work that no one taught you how to do.

The ones healing wounds you didn't cause.

The ones choosing presence over patterns, peace over performance, and purpose over perfection.

You are the bridges between what was and what can be.

You are the wild hope your ancestors never dreamed to name.

You are proof that it's possible to begin again—and again.

May this book be a companion on your journey, a reminder that you are not alone in the messy middle, and that the river of your life still holds beauty, meaning, and momentum—no matter where you start.

We may never get it perfect. But we keep flowing forward.

And that, in itself, is sacred.

Resources

These are some of the books and ideas that inspired me or that I directly referenced in the preceding pages. They're worth exploring if you'd like to dive deeper into the science and stories that shaped this book.

INTRODUCTION

Bruce Feiler, *Life Is in the Transitions: Mastering Change at Any Age* (Penguin Press, 2020).

Wallace J. Nichols, *Blue Mind: The Surprising Science That Shows How Being Near, In, On, or Under Water Can Make You Happier, More Connected, and Better at What You Do* (Little, Brown and Company, 2014).

Philip Brickman and Donald T. Campbell, "Hedonic Relativism and Planning the Good Society," in *Adaptation-Level Theory*, edited by M. H. Appley (Academic Press, 1971).

Michael Easter, *The Comfort Crisis: Embrace Discomfort to Reclaim Your Wild, Happy, Healthy Self* (Rodale Books, 2021).

CHAPTER 1

Brené Brown, *Dare to Lead: Brave Work. Tough Conversations. Whole Hearts.* (Random House, 2018).

Thich Nhat Hanh, *Peace Is Every Step: The Path of Mindfulness in Everyday Life* (Bantam Books, 1992).

CHAPTER 2

Matt Kahn, *Whatever Arises, Love That: A Love Revolution That Begins with You* (Sounds True, 2016).

Kristin Neff, *Self-Compassion: The Proven Power of Being Kind to Yourself* (William Morrow, 2015).

Desmond Tutu and Mpho Tutu, *The Book of Forgiving: The Fourfold Path for Healing Ourselves and Our World* (HarperOne, 2014).

CHAPTER 3

Bruce Feiler, *Life Is in the Transitions: Mastering Change at Any Age* (Penguin Press, 2020).

Abraham H. Maslow, "A Theory of Human Motivation," *Psychological Review* 50, no. 4 (1943): 370–96.

CHAPTER 4

Brené Brown, *Daring Greatly: How the Courage to Be Vulnerable Transforms the Way We Live, Love, Parent, and Lead* (Gotham Books, 2012).

Brené Brown, *Dare to Lead: Brave Work. Tough Conversations. Whole Hearts.* (Random House, 2018).

Brené Brown, *Rising Strong: How the Ability to Reset Transforms the Way We Live, Love, Parent, and Lead* (Spiegel & Grau, 2015).

Kristin Neff, *Self-Compassion: The Proven Power of Being Kind to Yourself* (William Morrow, 2015).

Kristin Neff, "Self-Compassion Test," Self-Compassion.org. Accessed 2025. https://self-compassion.org/self-compassion-test/

Ellen J. Langer, *Mindfulness* (Da Capo Press, 1989).

CHAPTER 5

Centers for Disease Control and Prevention, "About Adverse Childhood Experiences (ACEs)," CDC.gov. Accessed 2025. https://www.cdc.gov/aces/about

Compassion Prison Project, "Step Inside the Circle," YouTube.com. Accessed 2025. https://www.youtube.com/watch?v=FVxjuTkWQiE

Brené Brown, *Atlas of the Heart: Mapping Meaningful Connection and the Language of Human Experience* (Random House, 2021).

Arthur C. Brooks, *From Strength to Strength: Finding Success, Happiness, and Deep Purpose in the Second Half of Life* (Portfolio, 2022).

Lynne Twist, *The Soul of Money: Reclaiming the Wealth of Our Inner Resources* (W. W. Norton, 2003).

Michael Easter, *Scarcity Brain: Fix Your Craving Mindset and Rewire Your Habits to Thrive with Enough* (Rodale, 2023).

CHAPTER 6

Daniel Goleman, *Emotional Intelligence: Why It Can Matter More Than IQ* (Bantam Books, 1995).

Antonio R. Damasio, *Descartes' Error: Emotion, Reason, and the Human Brain* (Putnam, 1994).

The Complete Leader, "The Complete Leader Program," *Thecompleteleader.org*. Accessed 2025. https://www.thecomplete-leader.org/leadership-development-program

Amy Wrzesniewski et al., "Jobs, Careers, and Callings: People's Relations to Their Work," *Journal of Research in Personality* 31, no. 1 (1997): 21–33.

Wayne Dyer, *You'll See It When You Believe It* (HarperOne, 1989).

Viktor E. Frankl, *Man's Search for Meaning* (Beacon Press, 2006).

The Feelings Wheel, Feelingswheel.com. Accessed 2025. https://feelingswheel.com/

Yale School of Medicine, "The How We Feel App: Helping Emotions Work for Us, Not Against Us," December 1, 2022. https://medicine.yale.edu/news-article/the-how-we-feel-app-helping-emotions-work-for-us-not-against-us/

Susan David, *Emotional Agility: Get Unstuck, Embrace Change, and Thrive in Work and Life* (Avery, 2016).

Brianna Wiest, *101 Essays That Will Change the Way You Think* (Thought Catalog Books, 2016).

Peter Crone, "The Mastermind with Peter Crone, the Mind Architect," Petercrone.com. Accessed 2025. https://www.petercrone.com/mastermind

CHAPTER 7

The Mel Robbins Podcast, "Why 80% of Autoimmune Diseases Happen to Women & Solutions From a Renowned MD," with Dr. Sara Szal.

Galit Atlas, *Emotional Inheritance: A Therapist, Her Patients, and the Legacy of Trauma* (Little, Brown Spark, 2022).

Rachel Yehuda et al., "Influences of Maternal and Paternal PTSD on Epigenetic Regulation of the Glucocorticoid Receptor Gene in Holocaust Survivor Offspring," *American Journal of Psychiatry* (2014).

Bessel van der Kolk, *The Body Keeps the Score: Brain, Mind, and Body in the Healing of Trauma* (Penguin Books, 2015).

Deb Dana, *Polyvagal Theory in Therapy: Engaging the Rhythm of Regulation* (W. W. Norton & Company, 2018).

CHAPTER 8

Modern Elder Academy (MEA), Meawisdom.com. Accessed 2025. https://www.meawisdom.com

Daniel H. Pink, *The Power of Regret: How Looking Backward Moves Us Forward* (Riverhead Books, 2022).

CHAPTER 9

Arthur C. Brooks, *From Strength to Strength: Finding Success, Happiness, and Deep Purpose in the Second Half of Life* (Portfolio, 2022).

Lisa Miller, *The Awakened Brain: The New Science of Spirituality and Our Quest for an Inspired Life* (Random House, 2021).

Cindy Wigglesworth, *SQ21: The Twenty-One Skills of Spiritual Intelligence* (SelectBooks, 2012).

Richard Rohr, *Falling Upward: A Spirituality for the Two Halves of Life* (Jossey-Bass, 2011).

CONCLUSION

Shelley Paxton, *Soulbbatical: A Corporate Rebel's Guide to Finding Your Best Life* (Simon & Schuster, 2020).

About the Author

Angie Lion is the co-founder and Chief Soul Officer of Black River Performance Management. As a business owner, speaker, facilitator, and author, her passion lies in helping people rise to their highest potential, embrace life's transitions, and lead with authenticity and love.

With over a decade of experience as a consultant, executive coach, and trainer, Angie has worked with leaders and organizations across industries to strengthen culture, unlock human potential, and navigate change with clarity and confidence. From national conferences and leadership symposiums to team retreats and workshops, she is known for blending engaging delivery, practical tools, and soulful insight that leave audiences inspired and equipped for real-world action.

Her journey has taken her from a challenging upbringing as the daughter of a young single mother, to the high-pressure environment of surgical suites, to stages and classrooms across the U.S. and beyond. Along the way, she has witnessed how the right blend of compassion and accountability can transform not only organizations, but lives.

As a recognized voice on emotional intelligence, authentic leadership, resilience, and human connection, Angie has been invited to speak for women's leadership conferences, nonprofit organizations, government agencies, and business associations. Her work has been described as both deeply engaging and immediately practical, giving people tools they can use to grow as leaders, teammates, and human beings.

She is especially passionate about mentoring women in business and advocating for underserved and minority entrepreneurs, using both her platform and lived experience to empower others to lead with courage and purpose.

Connect With Me

★ ★ ★ ★ ★

Love This Book . . . Give a 5-Star Review

If you enjoyed this book, leave a five-star review on Amazon
and help others discover it. Your review is invaluable.

Gift a Book

Gifting a book, ebook, or audiobook could change someone's life. You
can gift a book on Amazon very easily.

Empower Your Team and Future Leaders

Purchase copies of this book as a powerful resource to help people
rise into their highest potential, embrace life's transitions, and lead with
authenticity and love. To order this book in bulk quantities,
email alohapublishing@gmail.com or visit AlohaBookStore.com

Invite Me to Speak

Interested in a speaking engagement at your company,
organization, or event? Connect with me at AngieLion.com

Discover Black River Performance Management

We are human systems architects committed to more than just
delivering training—we partner with leaders to reimagine and reconstruct
the way they work. For more information, visit BlackRiverPM.com

Growth happens outside of our comfort zones. Bravery happens when you make a choice to move forward even while scared.

www.ingramcontent.com/pod-product-compliance
Lightning Source LLC
Chambersburg PA
CBHW071731200326

41519CB00021BC/6671